Dedication

To all children who love to explore the world of imagination anda creativity. May this coloring book bring joy and fun, filling yours lives with vibrant colors and endless adventures. May each page be an invitation to dream, create and marvel. with love and affection.

Claudia Modesto

Presentation

The Animals in Noah's Ark – Coloring Book

In ancient times, when the earth was filled with wickedness, God chose a righteous man named Noah for a very special mission. He was given a divine command to build a great ark, a safe refuge for himself, his family, and the animals that God would send.

With obedience and faith, Noah worked tirelessly, and when the ark was ready, God sent the animals—a pair of each species. The majestic lions roared, the tiny birds fluttered in, the elephants marched with their trunks raised, the zebras entered side by side, and even the turtles crawled slowly but surely toward safety.

The rain began to fall, covering the entire earth, but inside the ark, there was safety, hope, and God's perfect plan. For forty days and forty nights, the ark floated upon the waters until, at last, the storm passed and life could begin anew. As a sign of God's promise, a beautiful rainbow appeared in the sky. Now, in this coloring book, you can bring this biblical story to life, coloring Noah, his family, and all the animals that found shelter in the ark! Use your imagination and embark on this incredible journey filled with faith, love, and colors!

Genesis 6-9 – The Story of Noah's Ark

ALL RIGHTS RESERVED ©

No part of this publication may be reproduced, distributed, or transmitted in any form or by any means, including photocopying, recording, or other electronic or mechanical methods, without the prior written permission of the publisher, except for brief quotations incorporated in critical reviews and other specific noncommercial uses. Any unauthorized replica of this work is prohibited.

C.M.©
Claudia Modesto's Publications

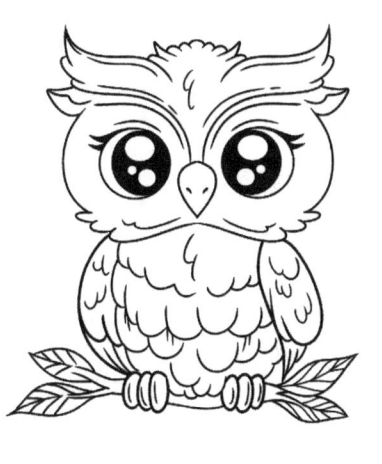
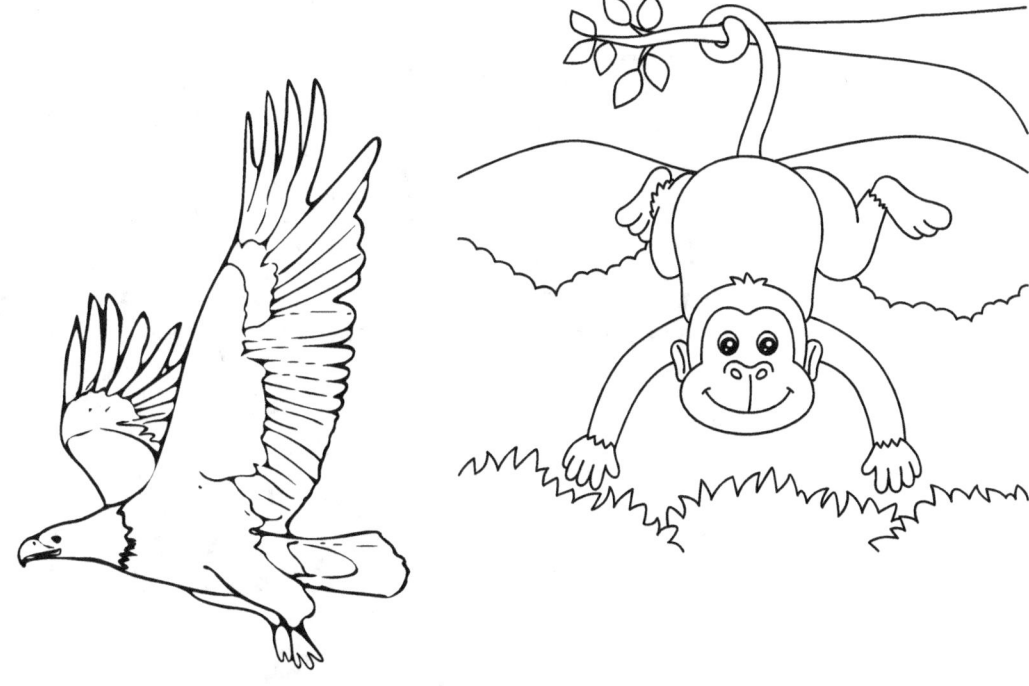

This Book Belongs To:

_____

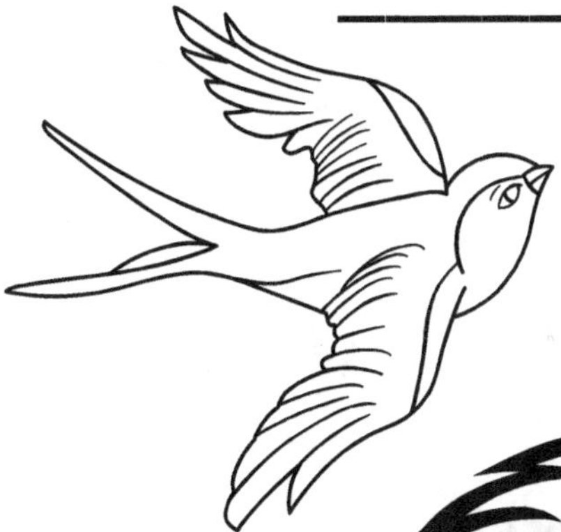

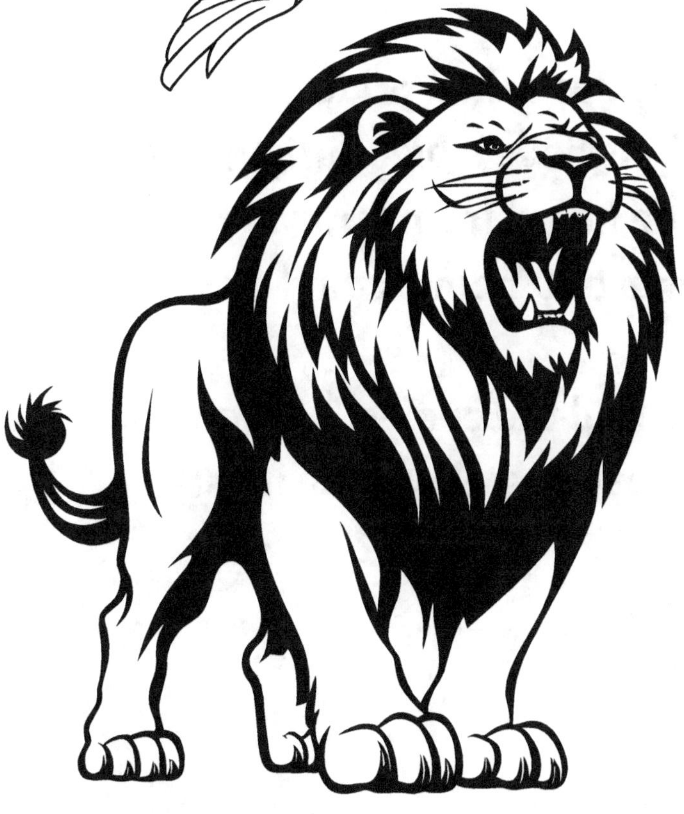

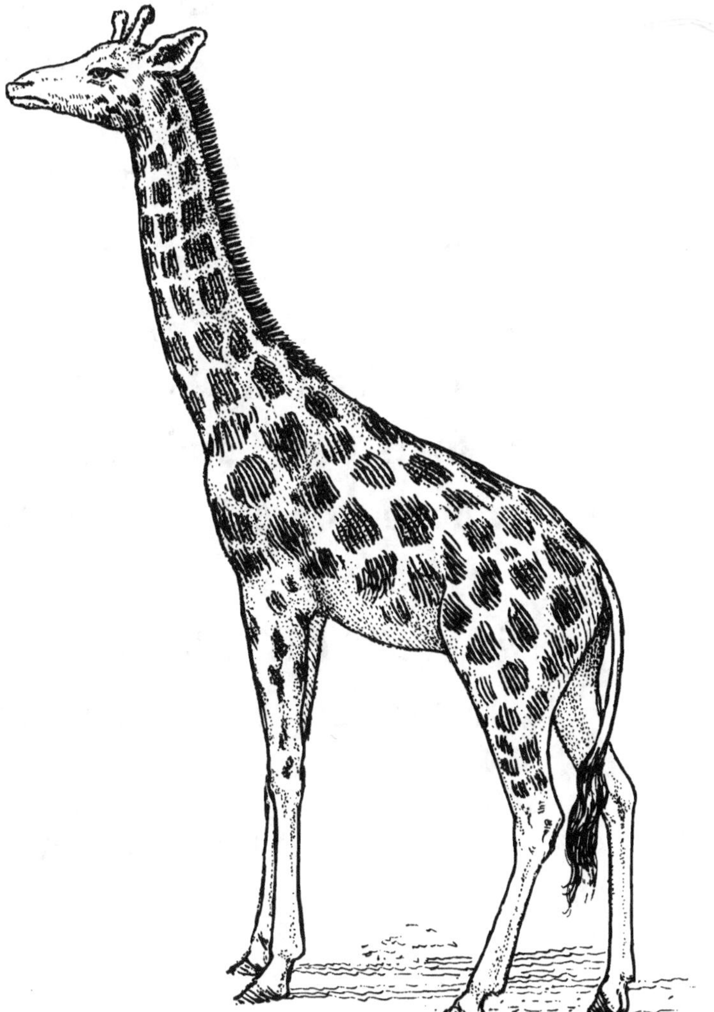

LION

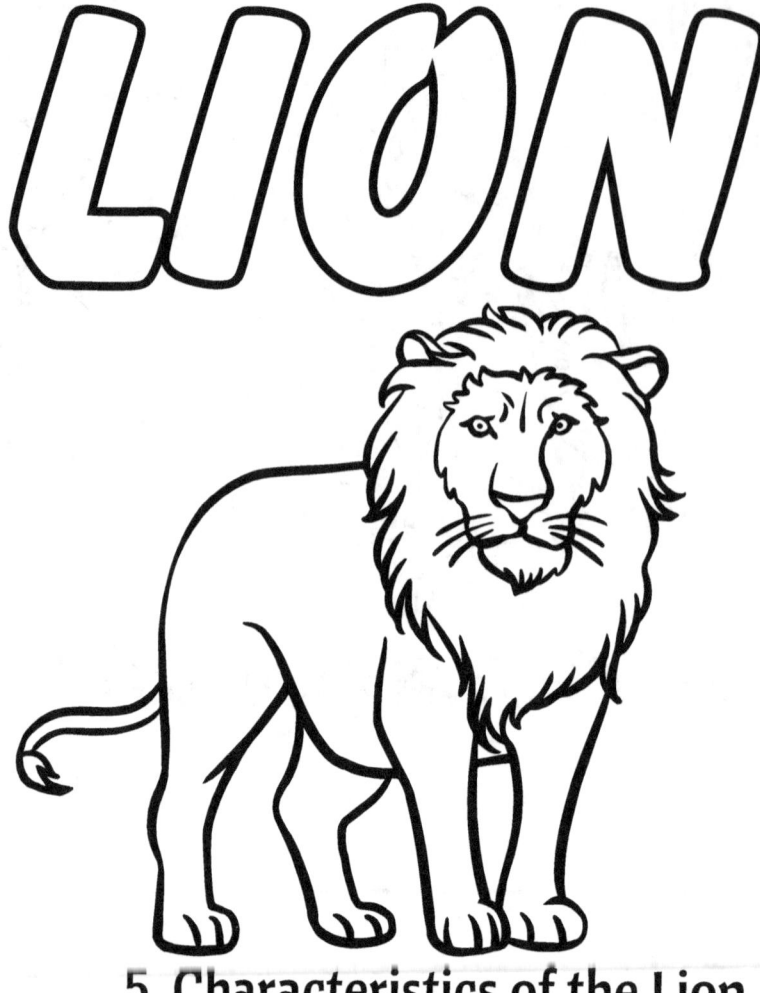

5 Characteristics of the Lion

1. Big and Strong – The lion is one of the most powerful animals in the savanna!
2. Lives with Family – It lives in groups called prides.
3. Has a Beautiful Mane – Male lions have a big, fluffy mane.
4. Roars Very Loud – Its roar can be heard from far away!
5. Loves to Rest – Lions sleep almost 20 hours a day!

Did you like it? Which fact did you find the coolest? Which of these characteristics did you like learning about the most?

Write the number here: _____

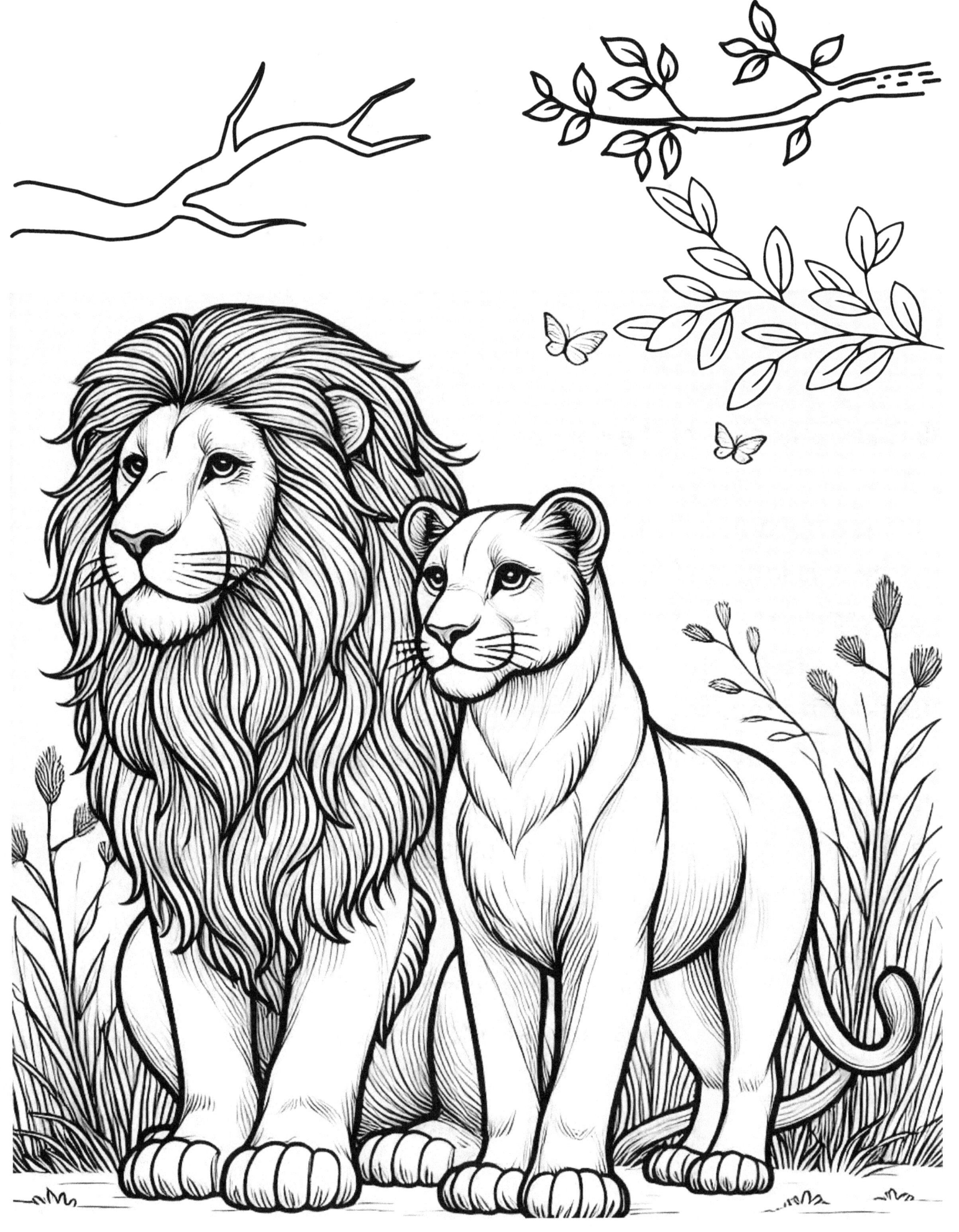

TOUCAN

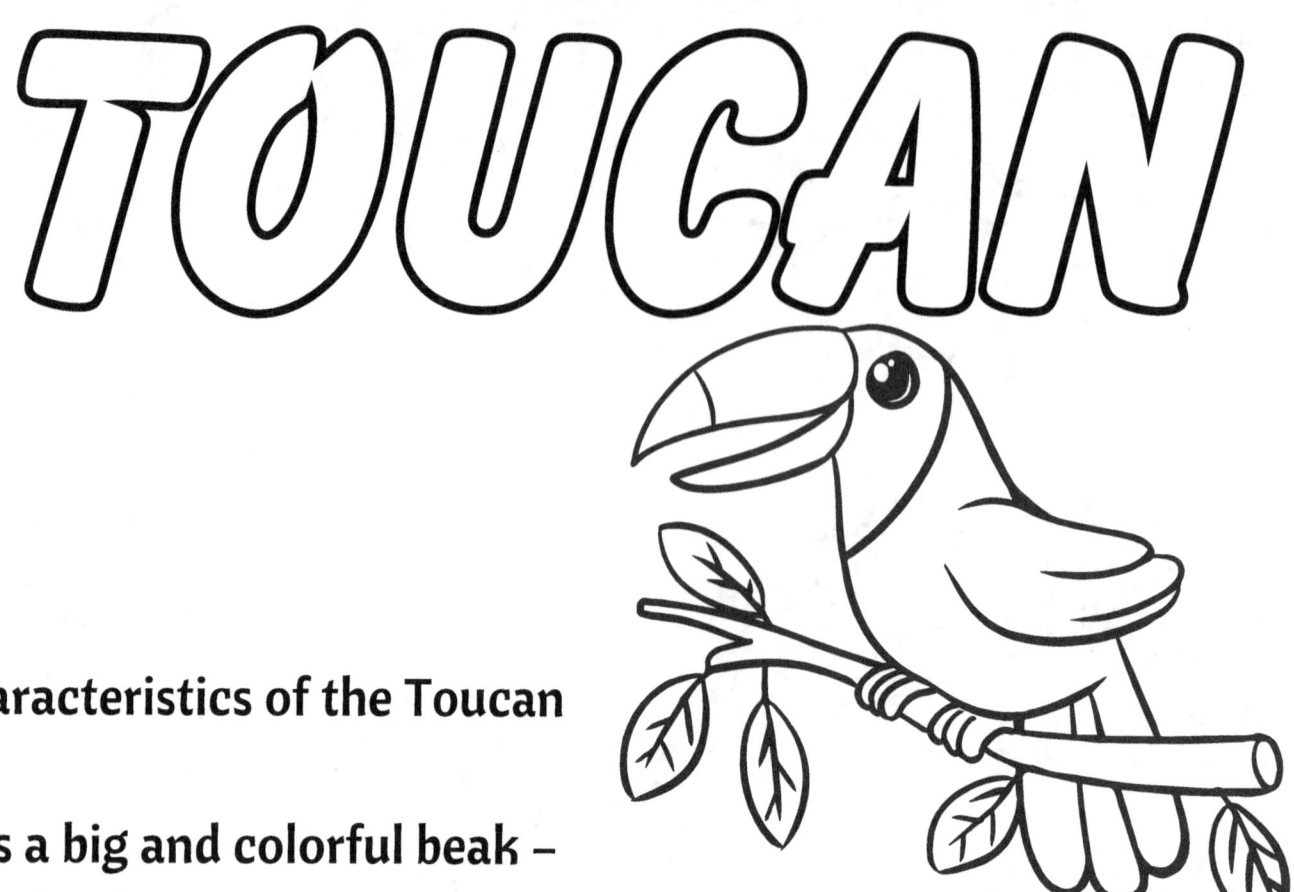

5 Characteristics of the Toucan

1. Has a big and colorful beak – Its beak is long and full of beautiful colors!
2. Lives in trees – It loves to stay on the branches in the forest.
3. .Loves to eat fruit – Its favorite food is fruit, but sometimes it eats insects too.
4. Makes funny sounds – Instead of singing like other birds, it makes popping or croaking noises.
5. Doesn't fly much – It prefers to hop from branch to branch instead of flying long distances.

Which of these characteristics did you like learning about the most?

Write the number here: _____

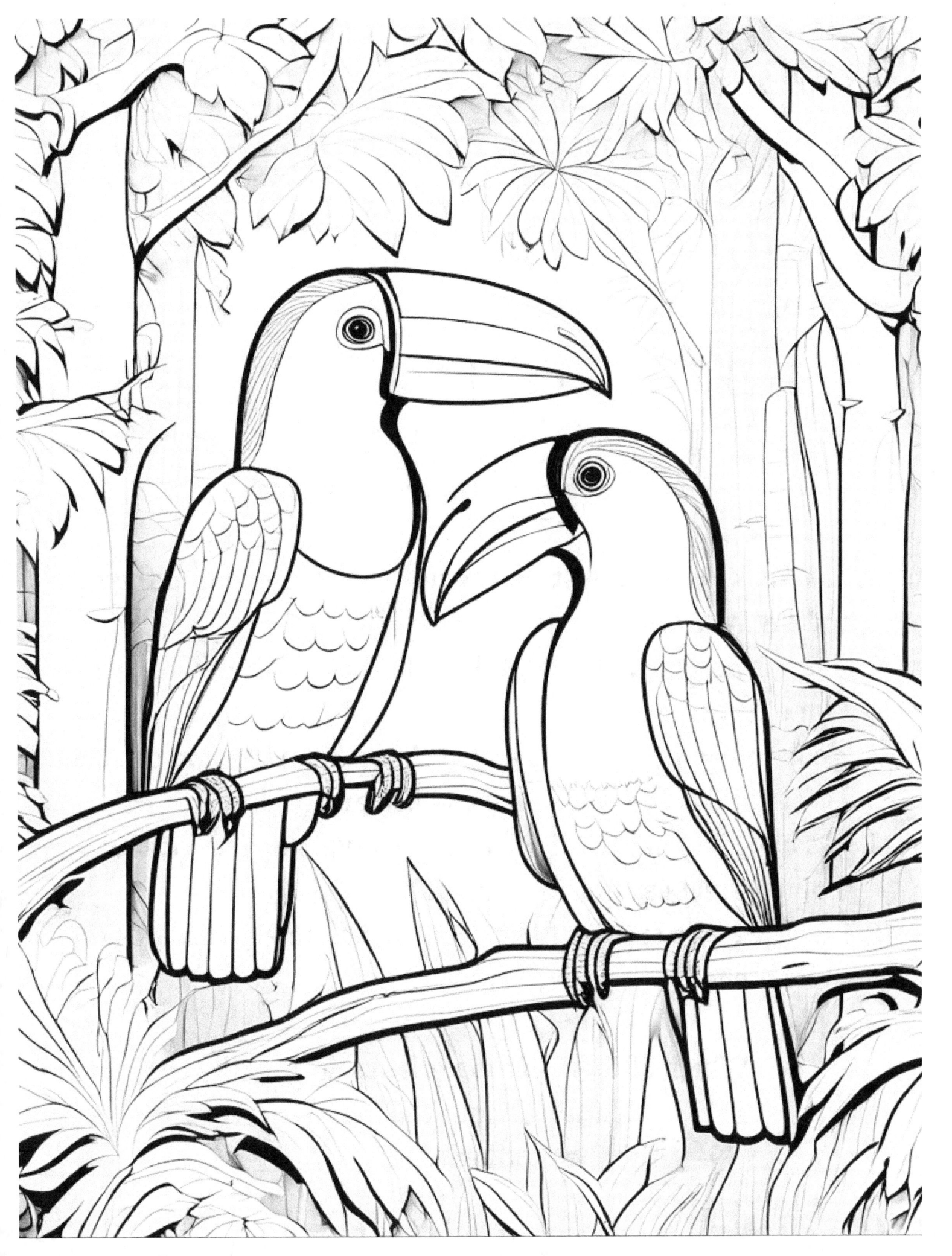

POLAR BEAR

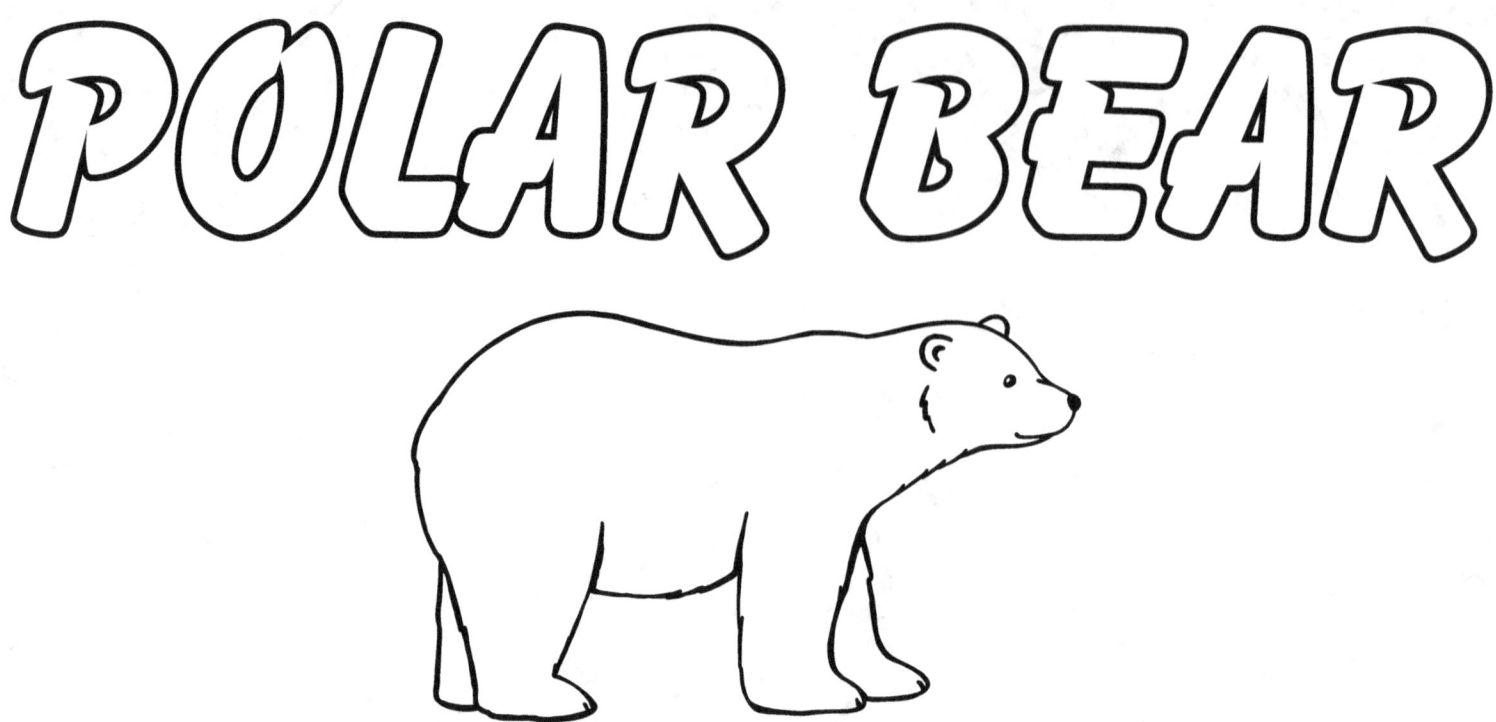

5 Characteristics of the Polar Bear

1. Has thick white fur – Its white fur helps it blend into the snow and stay warm.
2. Lives in very cold places – It lives in the Arctic, where there is a lot of snow and ice.
3. Is a great swimmer – It is an excellent swimmer and can spend a long time in the water hunting fish and seals.
4. Has big, furry paws – Its paws help it walk on ice without slipping and keep warm in the cold.
5. Eats a lot – To survive the extreme cold, it needs to eat a lot and store fat in its body.

Which of these characteristics did you like learning about the most?
Write the number here: _____

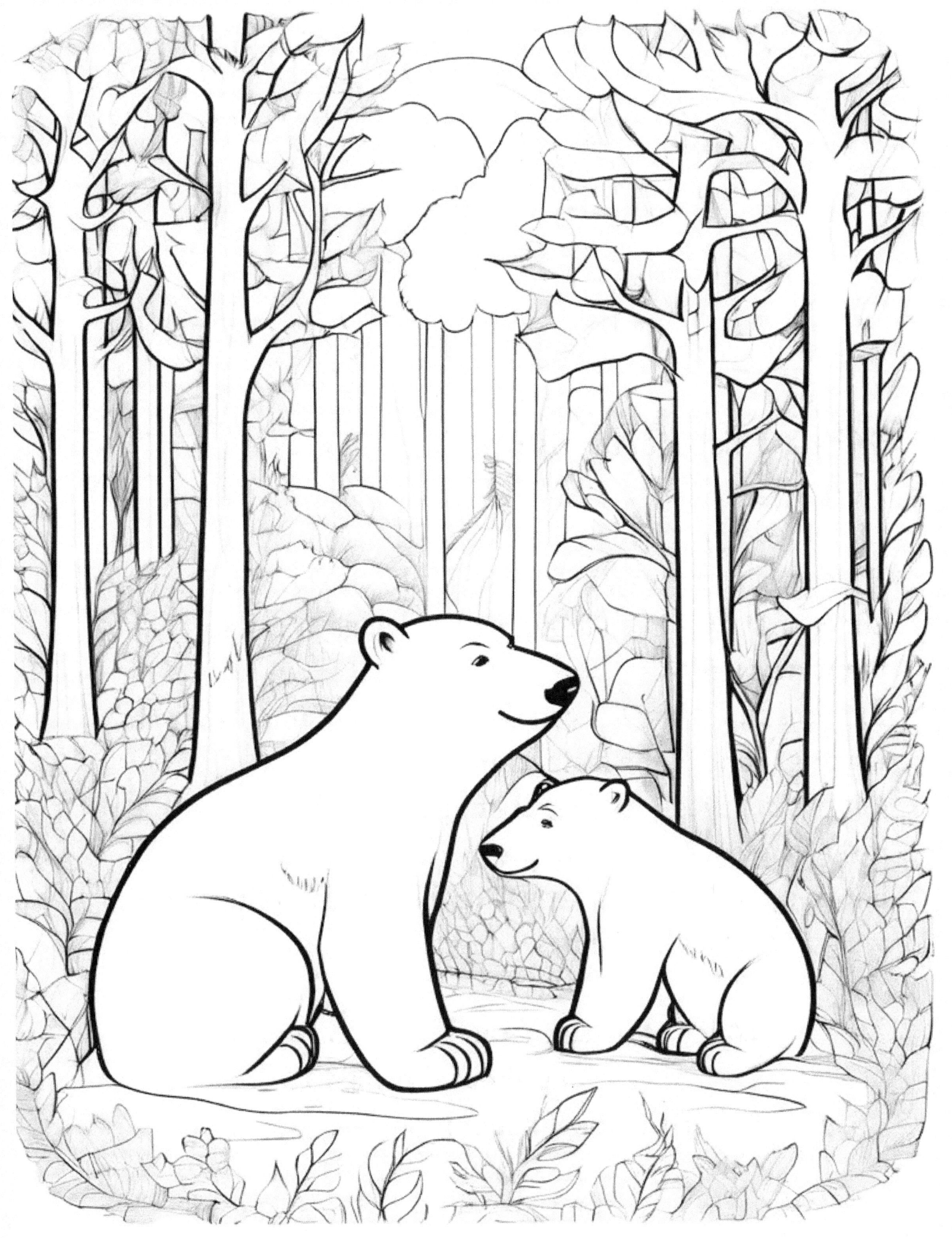

OSTRICH

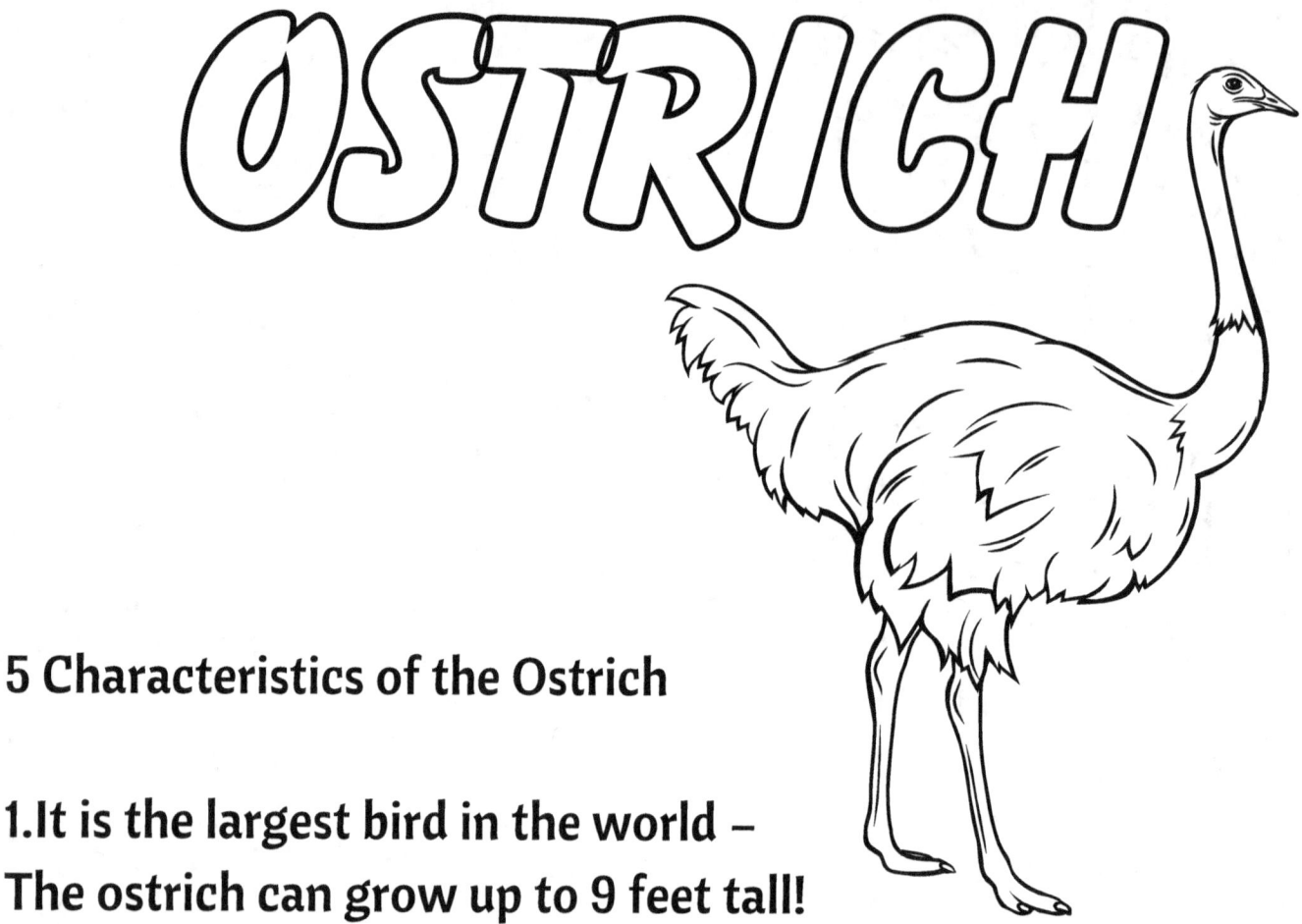

5 Characteristics of the Ostrich

1. It is the largest bird in the world – The ostrich can grow up to 9 feet tall!
2. It cannot fly – Even though it has wings, it cannot fly, but it runs very fast.
3. It runs super fast – It can reach speeds of up to 43 mph, making it one of the fastest birds.
4. It has big eyes – Its eyes are huge and help it see dangers from far away.
5. It lays giant eggs – Its eggs are the largest in the world, weighing up to 3.3 pounds.

Which of these characteristics did you like learning about the most?
Write the number here: _____

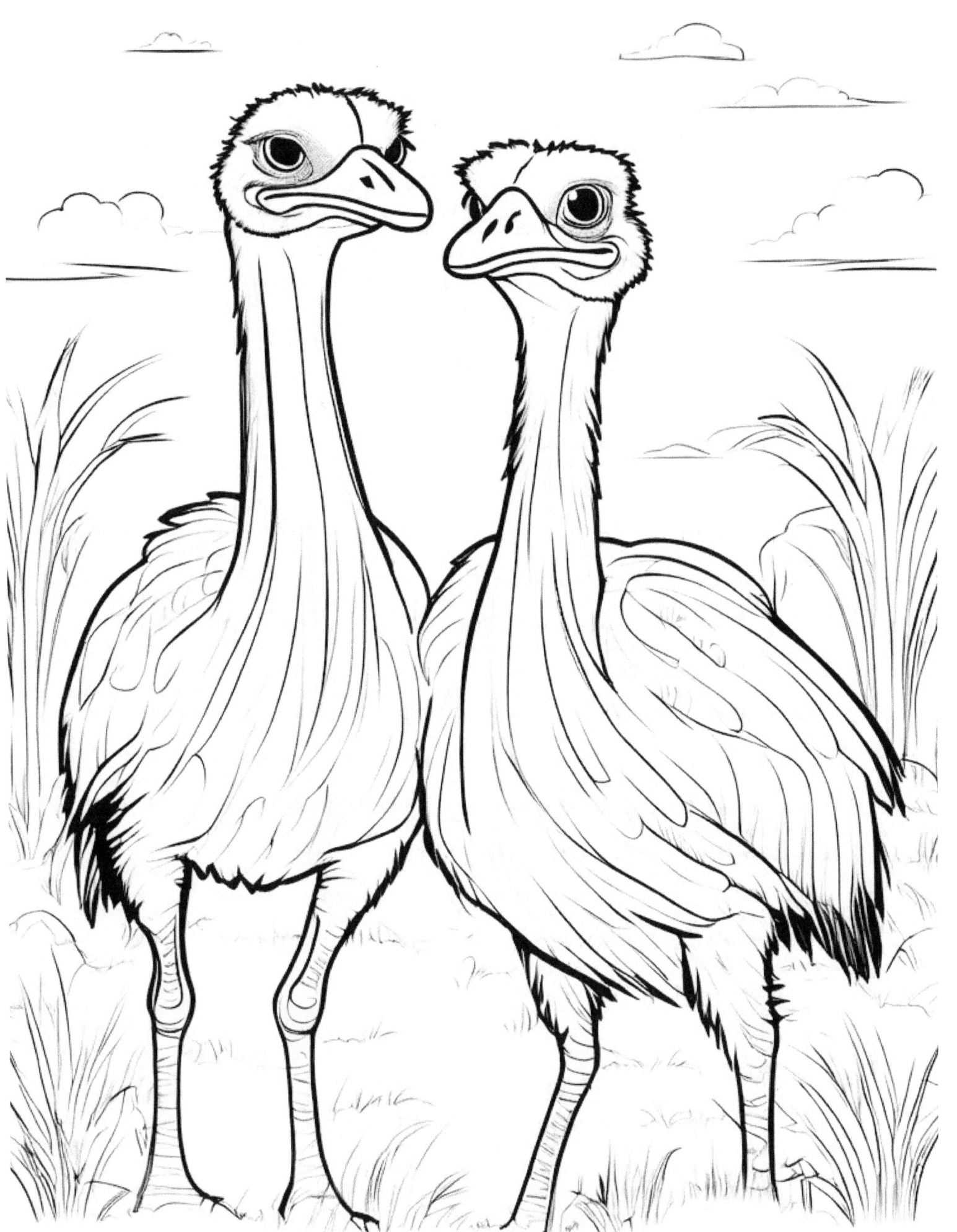

ZEBRA

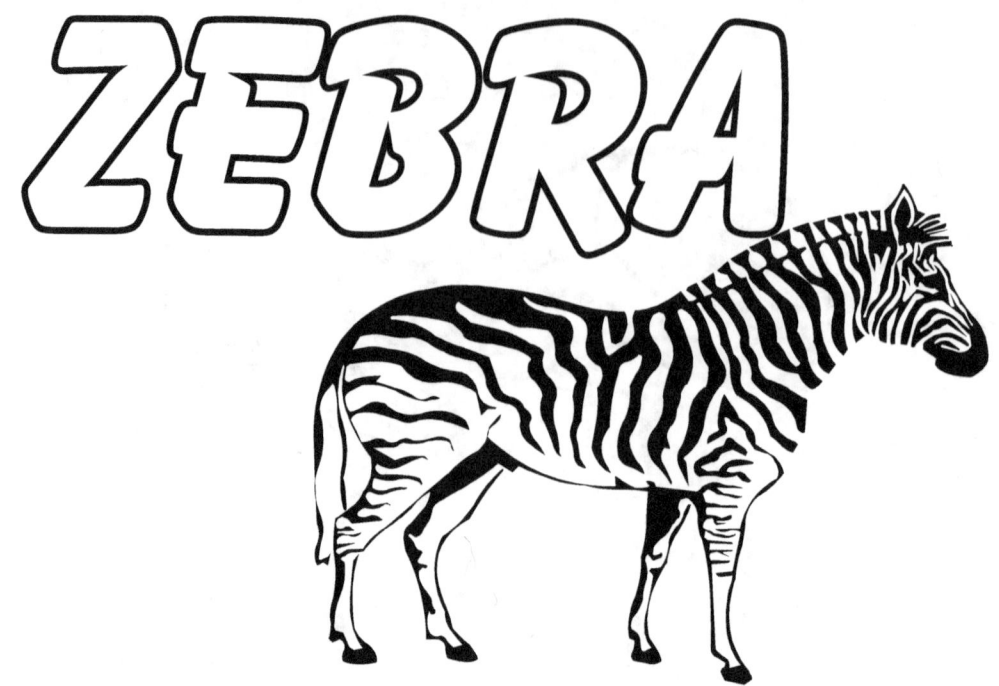

5 Characteristics of the Zebra

1. Has unique stripes – No zebra has the same stripes, each one has a different pattern.
2. Runs very fast – It can reach up to 40 mph to escape from predators.
3. Lives in groups – Zebras like to live in herds for protection.
4. Has great vision and hearing – Their eyes and ears help them spot danger from far away.
5. Communicates in many ways – They use sounds, ear movements, and even facial expressions to communicate.

Which of these characteristics did you like learning about the most?
Write the number here: _____

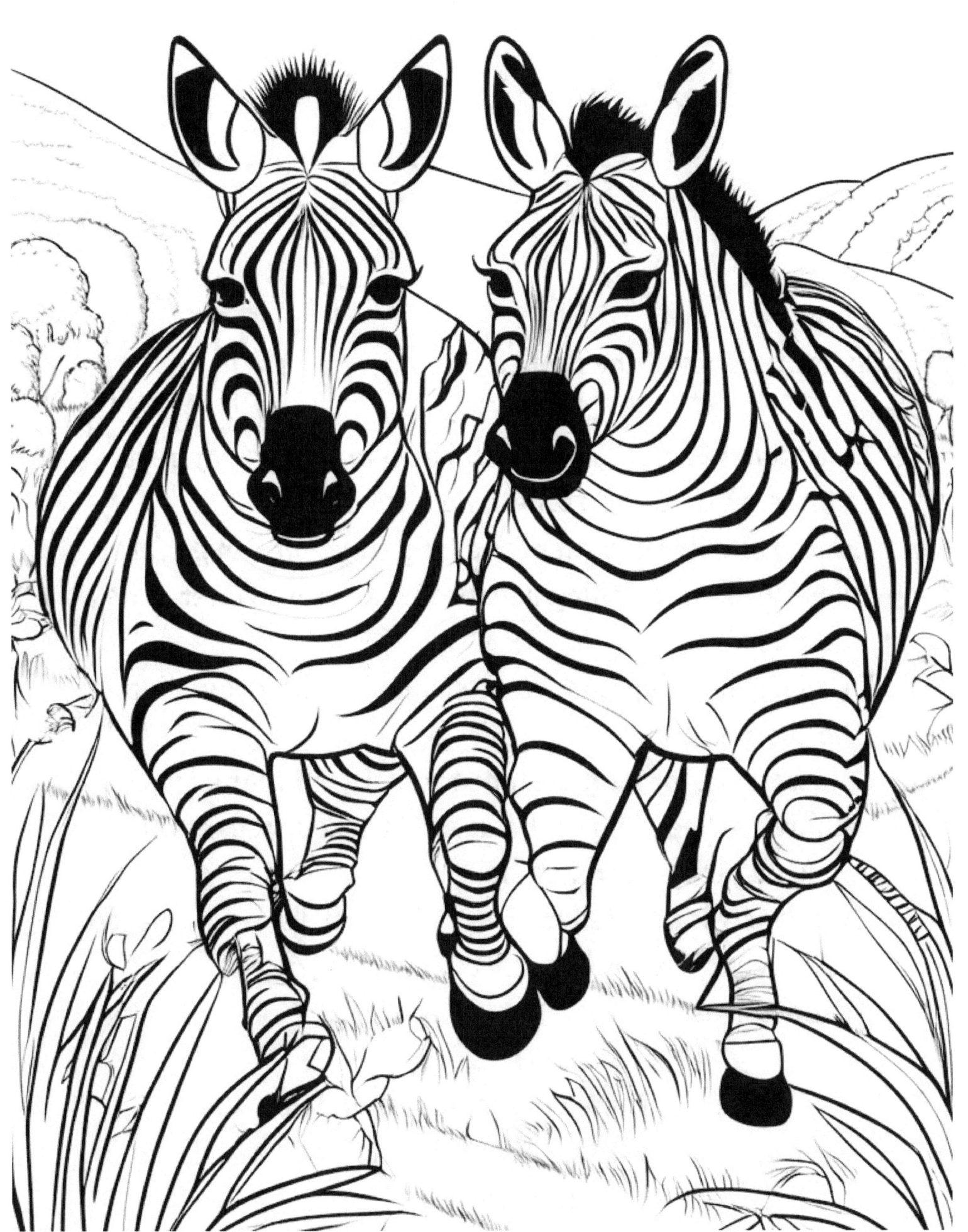

CAMEL

5 Characteristics of the Camel

1. Has two humps – The camel has two humps where it stores fat to feed on when there is no food.
2. Can live without water for a long time – It can go for days without drinking because it can store water in its body.
3. Has desert-adapted feet – Its wide feet help it walk on hot, loose sand.
4. Is excellent for long-distance travel – The camel is known as the "ship of the desert" because it can travel long distances carrying loads.
5. Has nostrils adapted for heat – Its nostrils can be closed to prevent sand and dust from entering during sandstorms.

Which of these characteristics did you like learning about the most?
Write the number here: _____

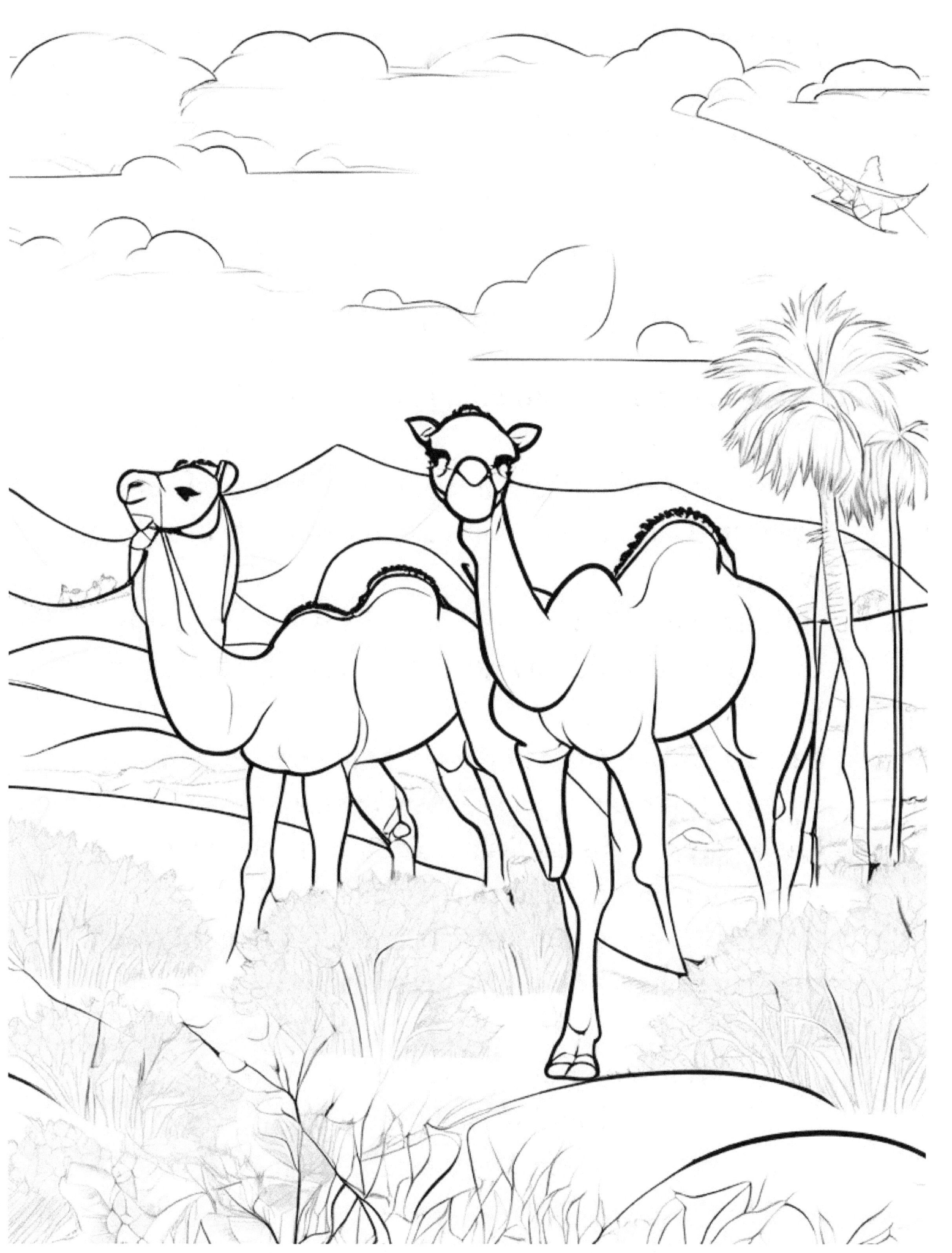

HUMMINGBIRD

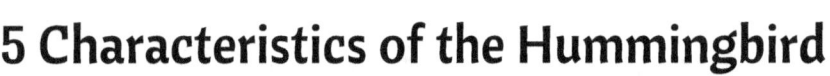

5 Characteristics of the Hummingbird

1. Can fly backward – The hummingbird is the only bird that can fly backward, thanks to the movement of its wings.
2. Has fast and agile flight – It beats its wings up to 80 times per second, allowing it to hover in the air for long periods.
3. Feeds on nectar from flowers – Its main food source is flower nectar, but it also eats small insects.
4. Has a very fast metabolism – To support all that energy, the hummingbird needs to eat many times a day.
5. Has bright colors – Its feathers are full of vibrant colors that can shine in the sunlight, especially on its chest.

Which of these characteristics did you like learning about the most?
Write the number here: _____

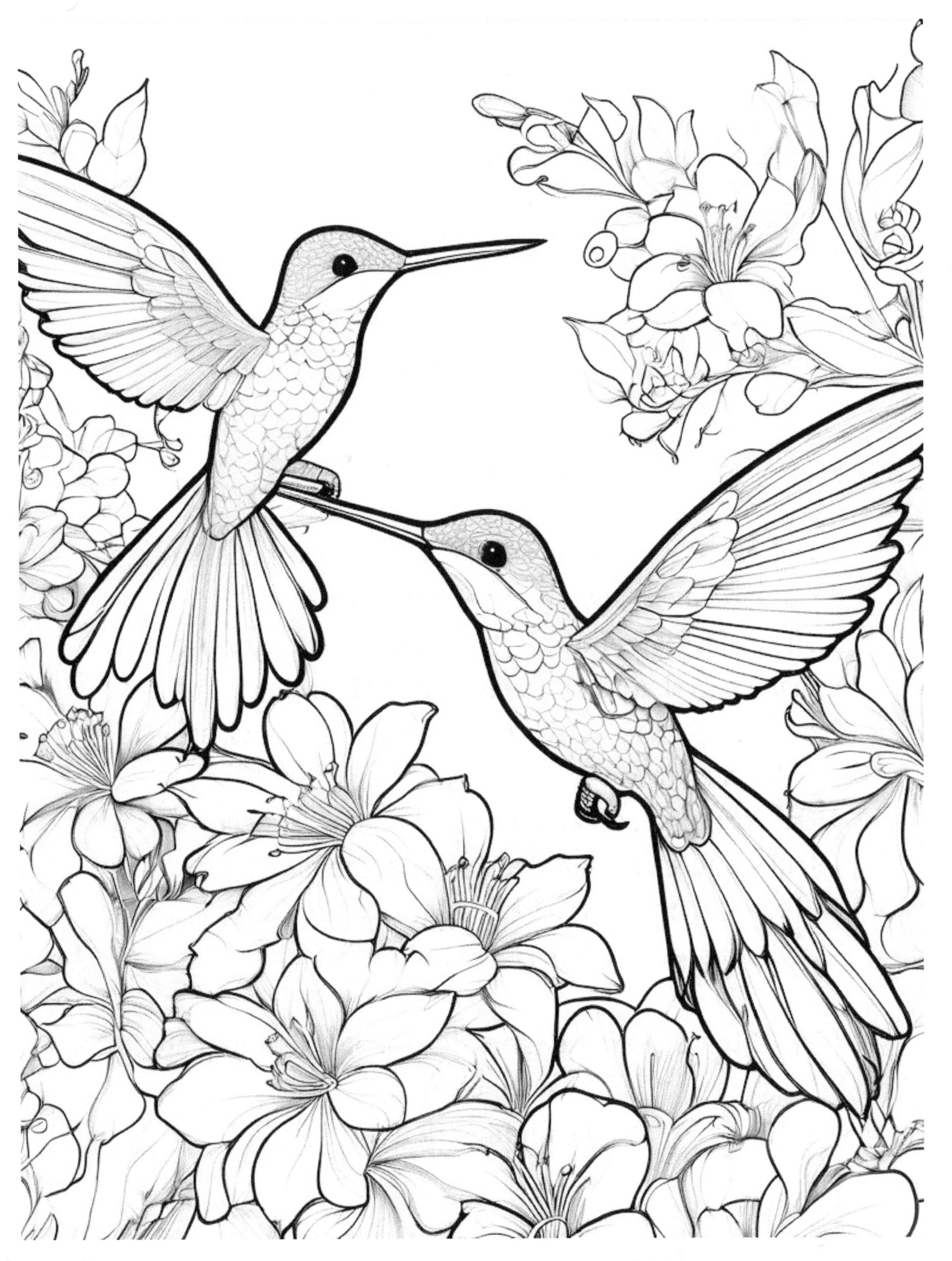

PARROT

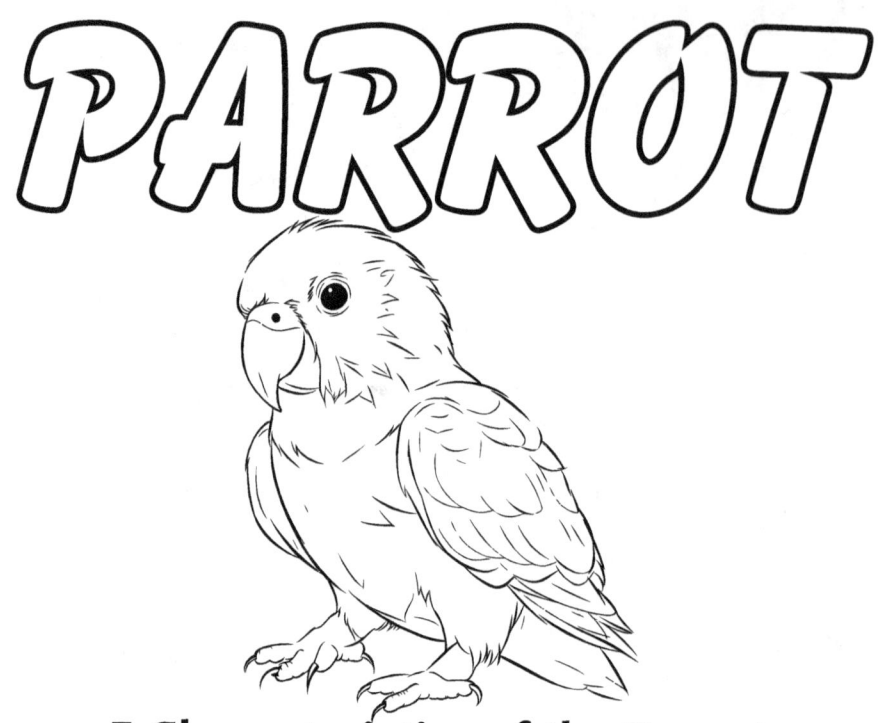

5 Characteristics of the Parrot

1. Is great at mimicking sounds – The parrot can imitate human voices and other sounds it hears.
2. Has colorful feathers – Its feathers are very vibrant, usually in shades of green, blue, red, and yellow.
3. Lives in groups – Parrots like to live in flocks, especially in tropical forests.
4. Eats fruits, seeds, and nuts – Its diet mainly consists of fruits and seeds, but it also eats some nuts.
5. Has a strong, curved beak – The parrot's beak is strong and adapted to crack seeds and open fruits.

Which of these characteristics did you like learning about the most?
Write the number here: _____

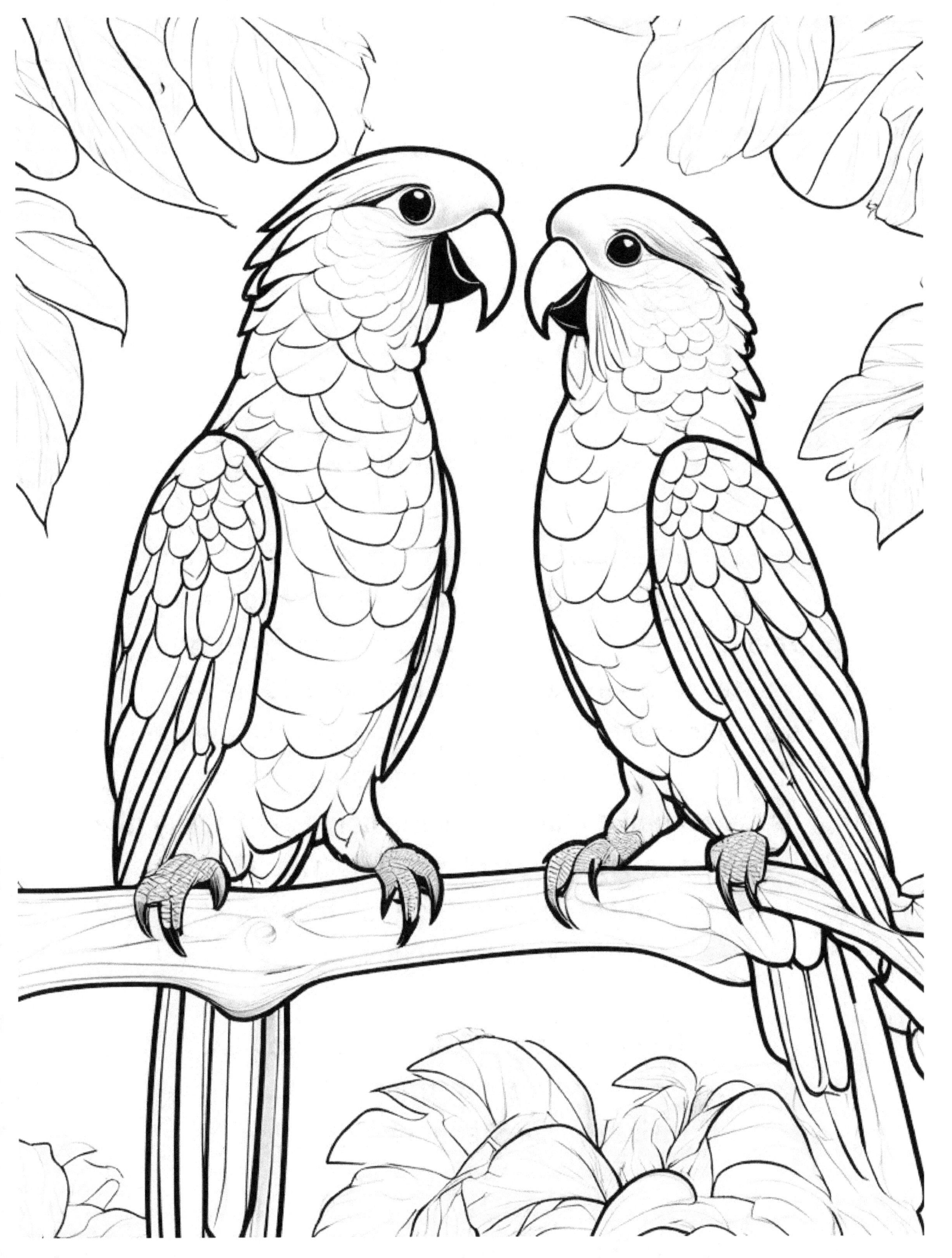

HIPPO

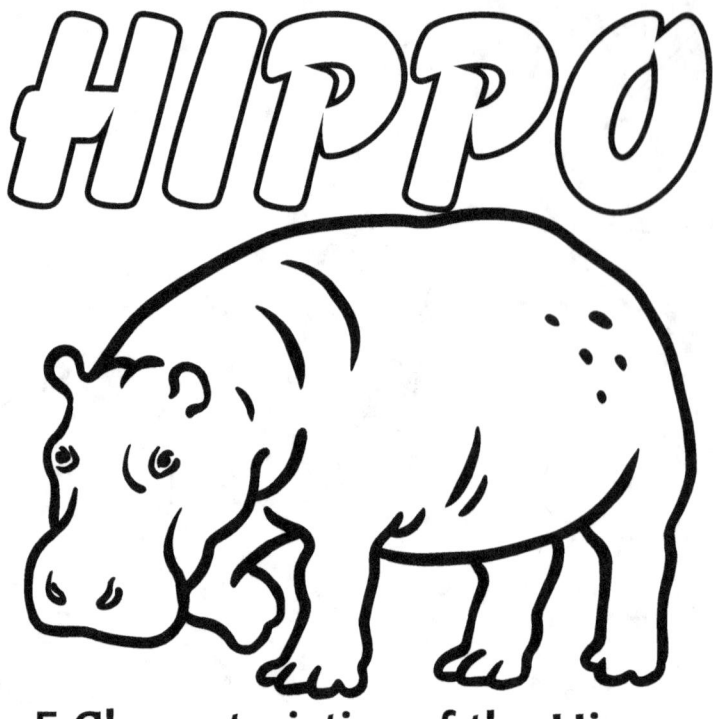

5 Characteristics of the Hippo

1. Is one of the largest land animals – The hippo can weigh up to 10,000 lbs and is very large and heavy.
2. Spends most of its time in water – It loves to swim and stay submerged in rivers and lakes to stay cool.
3. Has a huge mouth – The hippo's mouth can open up to 5 feet wide and has large, sharp teeth.
4. Is faster than it looks – Despite being very heavy, the hippo can run up to 19 mph for short distances.
5. Is herbivorous – The hippo mainly feeds on grass and plants found on land.

Which of these characteristics did you like learning about the most?
Write the number here: _____

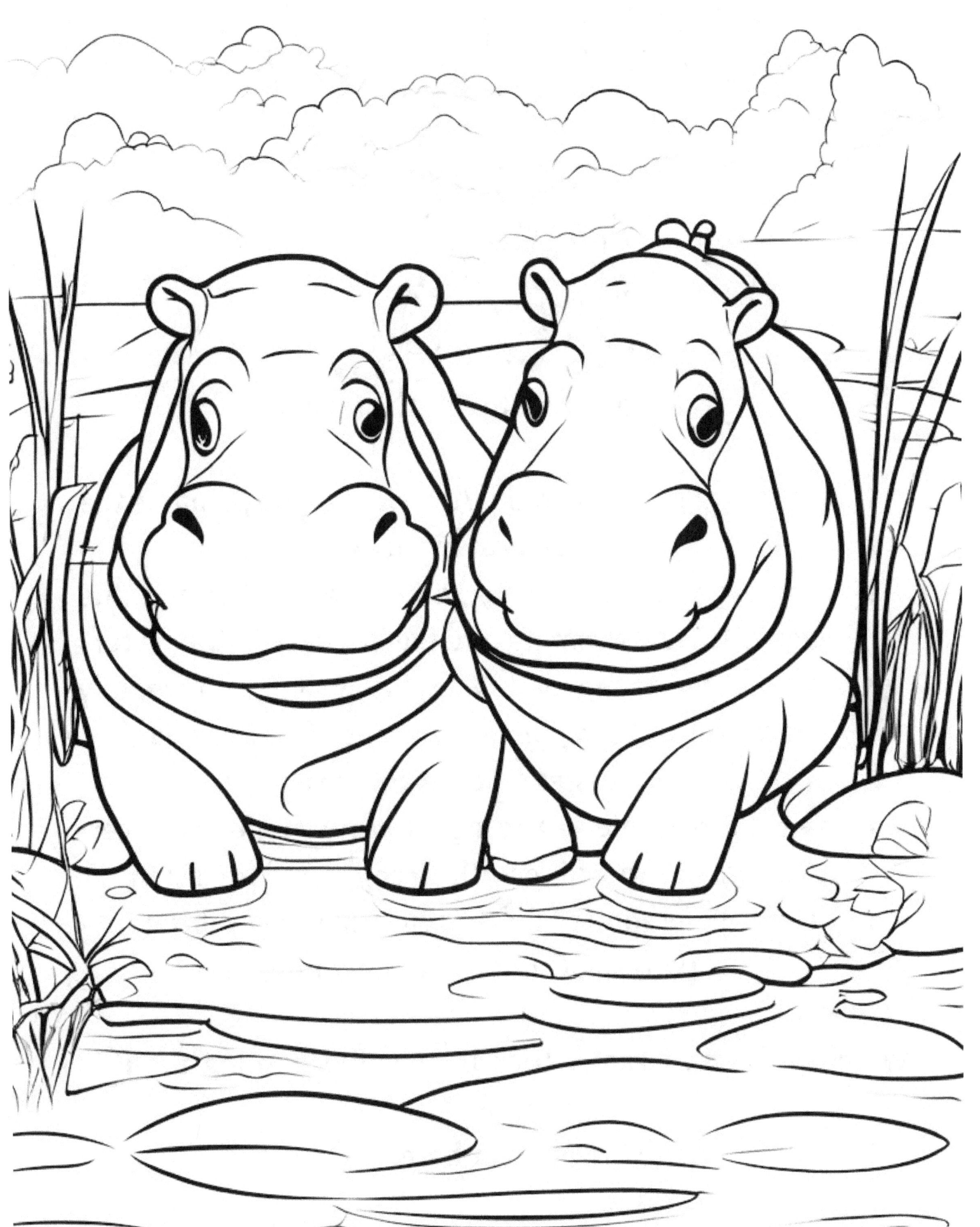

JAGUAR

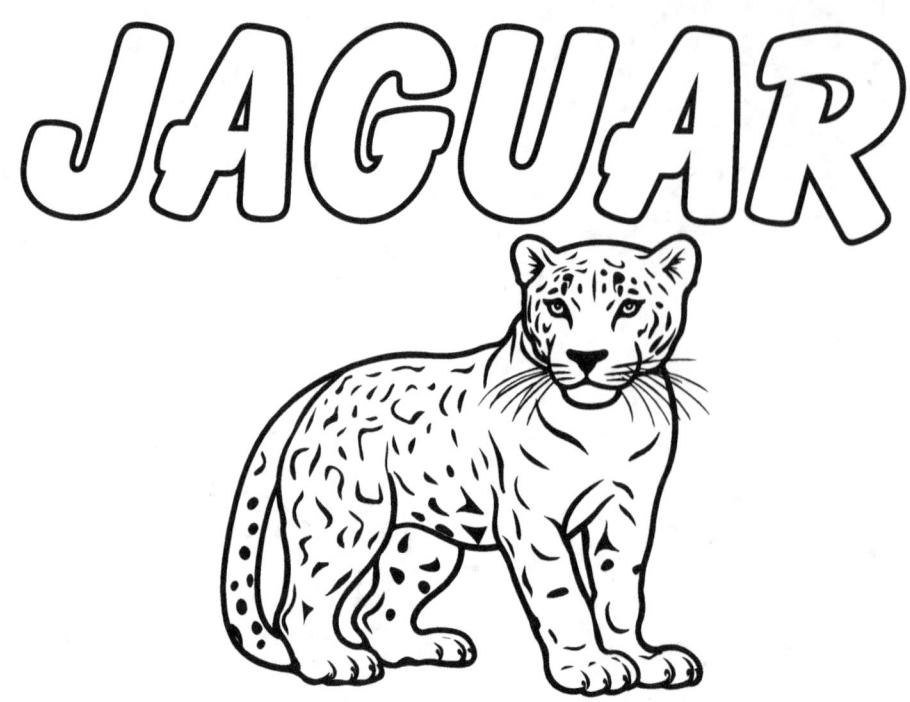

5 Characteristics of the Jaguar

1. **Is the largest feline in the Americas** – The jaguar is the largest wild cat in the Americas.
2. **Is an excellent swimmer** – Unlike many other cats, the jaguar loves swimming and feels at ease in the water.
3. **Has a super strong bite** – The jaguar's bite is incredibly powerful and can pierce the shells of turtles and the bones of large animals.
4. **Is a solitary hunter** – The jaguar hunts alone and is very strategic, attacking with strength and precision.
5. **Has unique spotted fur** – Each jaguar has a different pattern of spots, making it unique.

Which of these characteristics did you like learning about the most?
Write the number here: _____

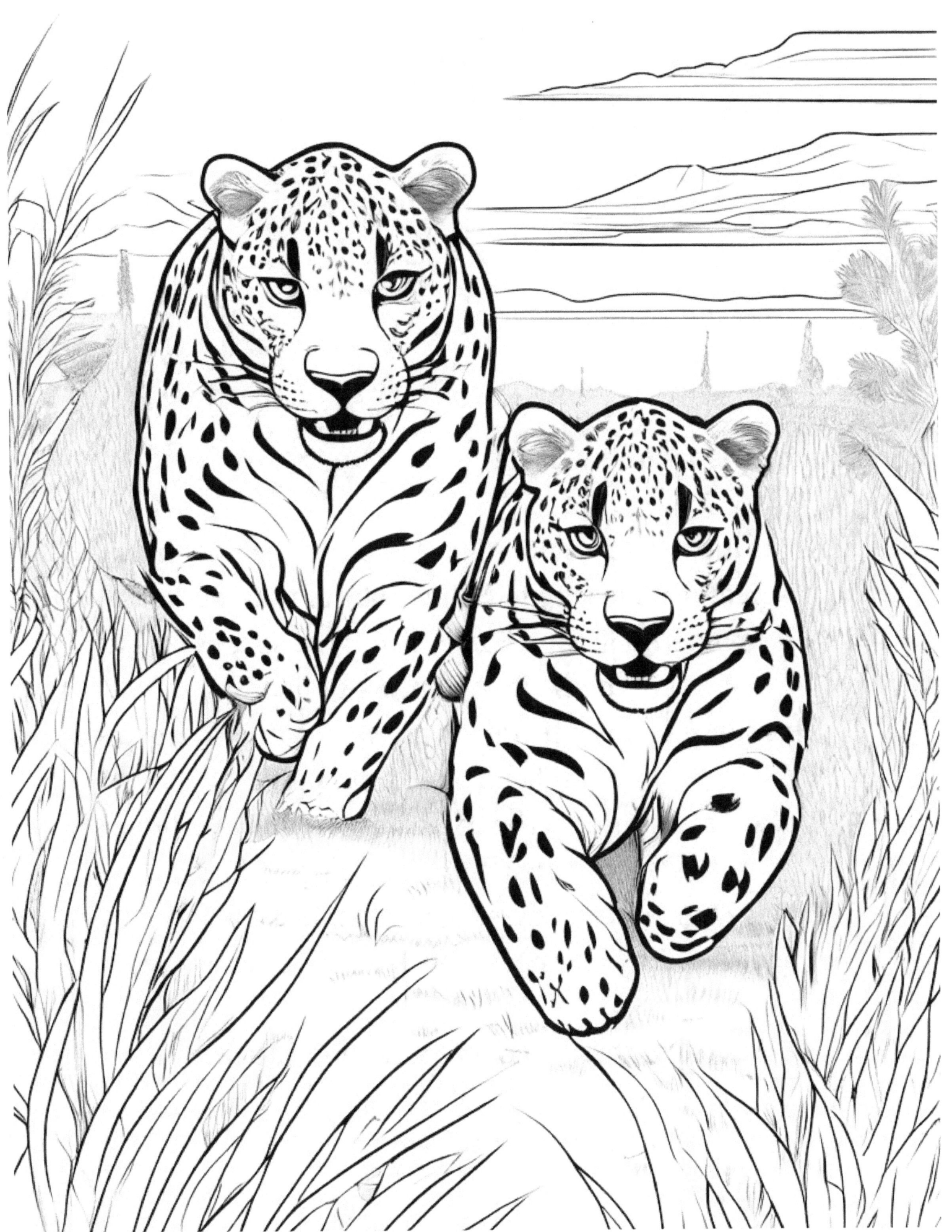

EAGLE

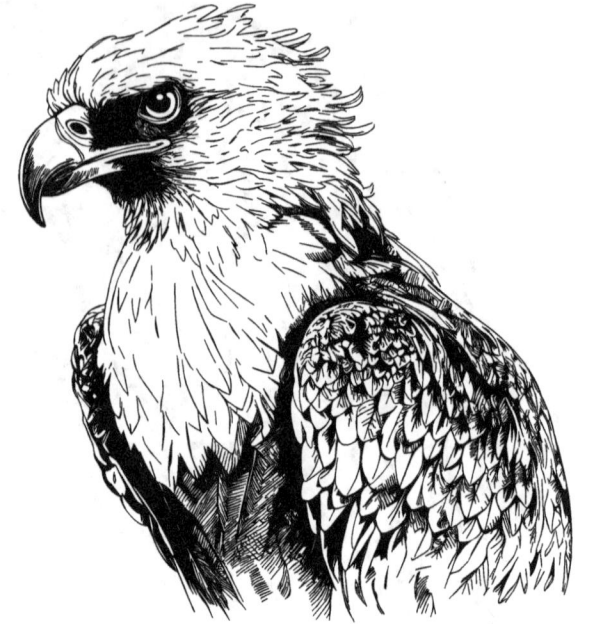

5 Characteristics of the Eagle

1. Has incredible vision – The eagle can see prey from a great distance, up to 8 times better than humans.
2. Has powerful flight – Eagles can fly at speeds of up to 100 mph when hunting or diving.
3. Has sharp talons – Its talons are strong and sharp, used to catch and hold onto prey.
4. Is a solitary hunter – The eagle hunts alone and typically feeds on small mammals, fish, and birds.
5. Builds huge nests – Eagles build their nests in large trees or cliffs, and these nests can be used for many years.

Which of these characteristics did you like learning about the most?
Write the number here: _____

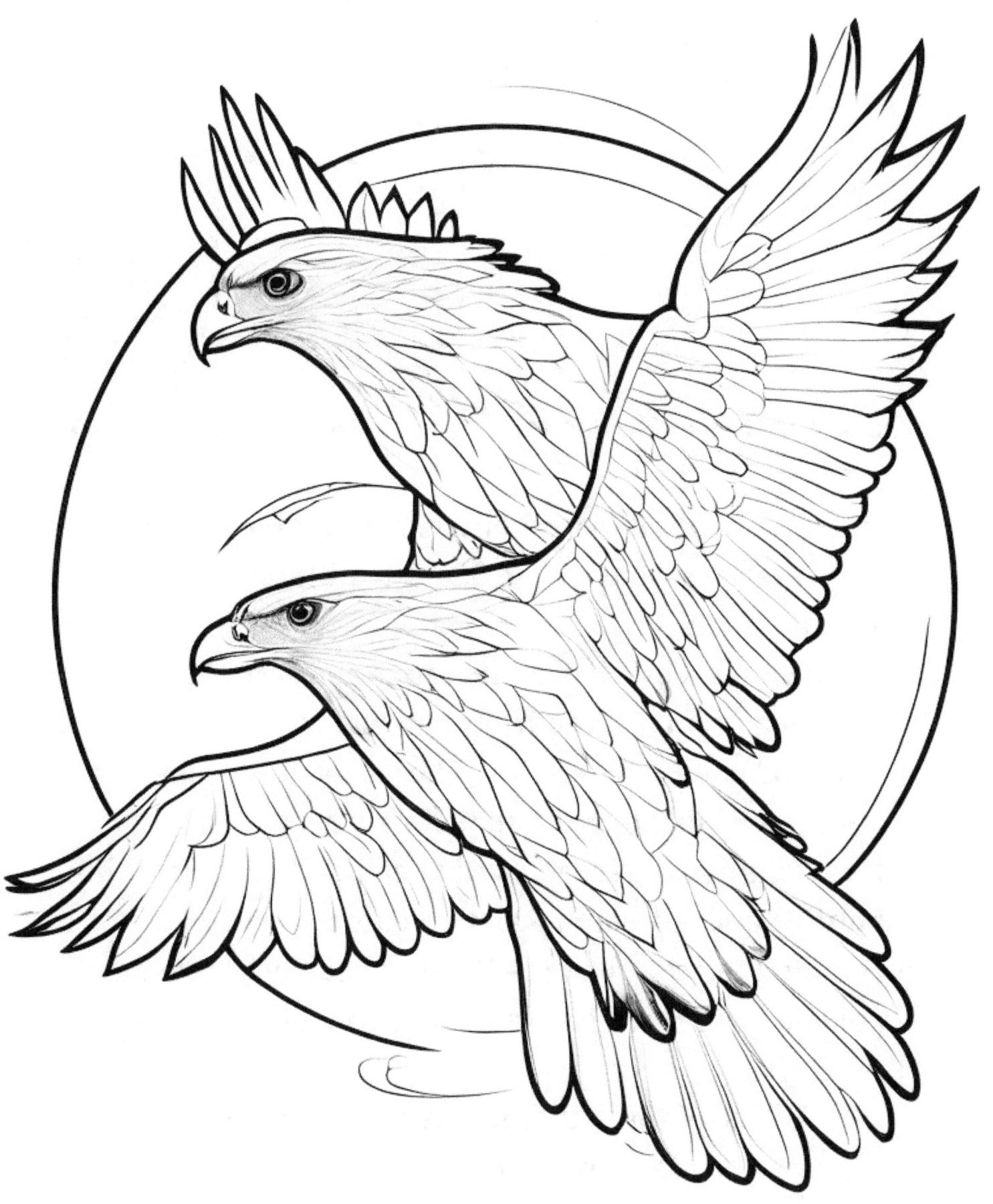

JACKAL

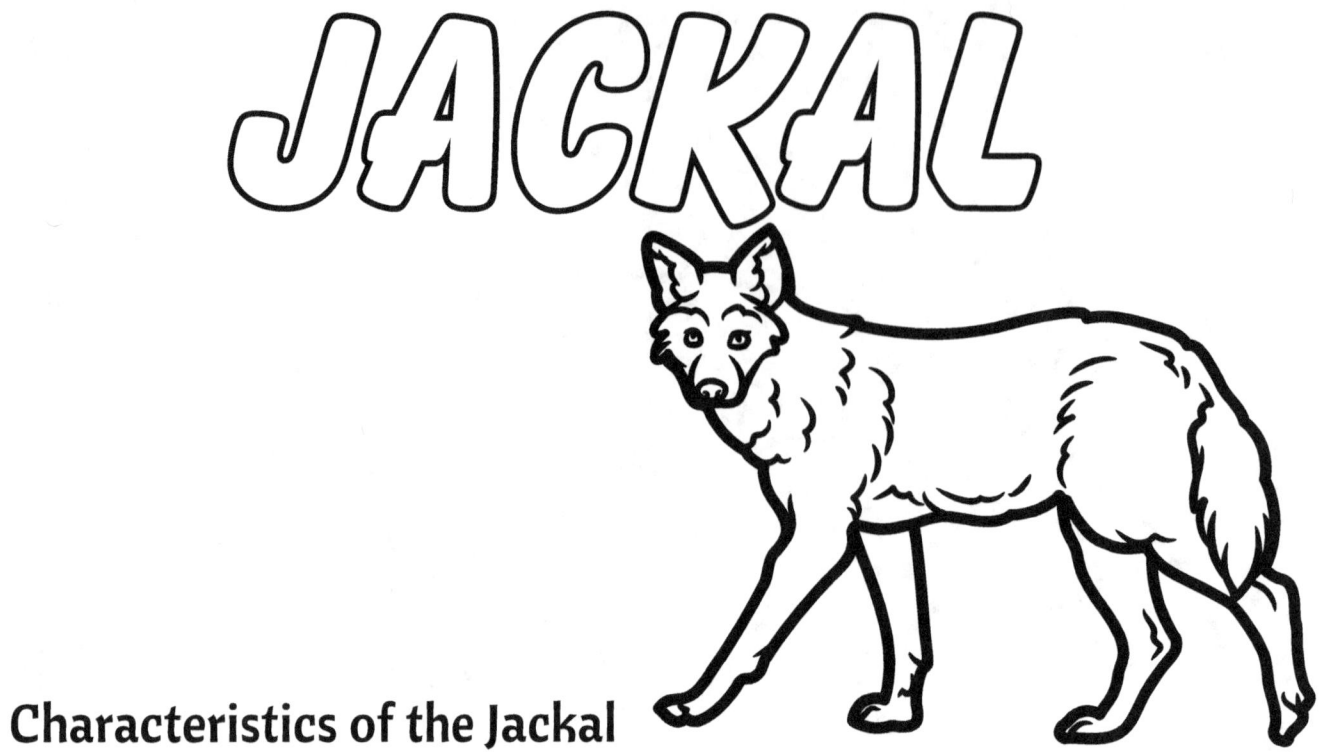

5 Characteristics of the Jackal

1. Is a very smart animal – The jackal is known for being very intelligent and able to adapt to different environments.
2. Has a varied diet – It is omnivorous and eats almost anything: from meat to fruits and plants.
3. Is a good nocturnal hunter – The jackal hunts mainly at night, using its sharp vision to locate prey.
4. Lives in groups – Jackals live in packs, which helps with hunting and protection from predators.
5. Has discreet-colored fur – Its fur is usually brown or golden, helping it blend into its surroundings.

Which of these characteristics did you like learning about the most?
Write the number here: _____

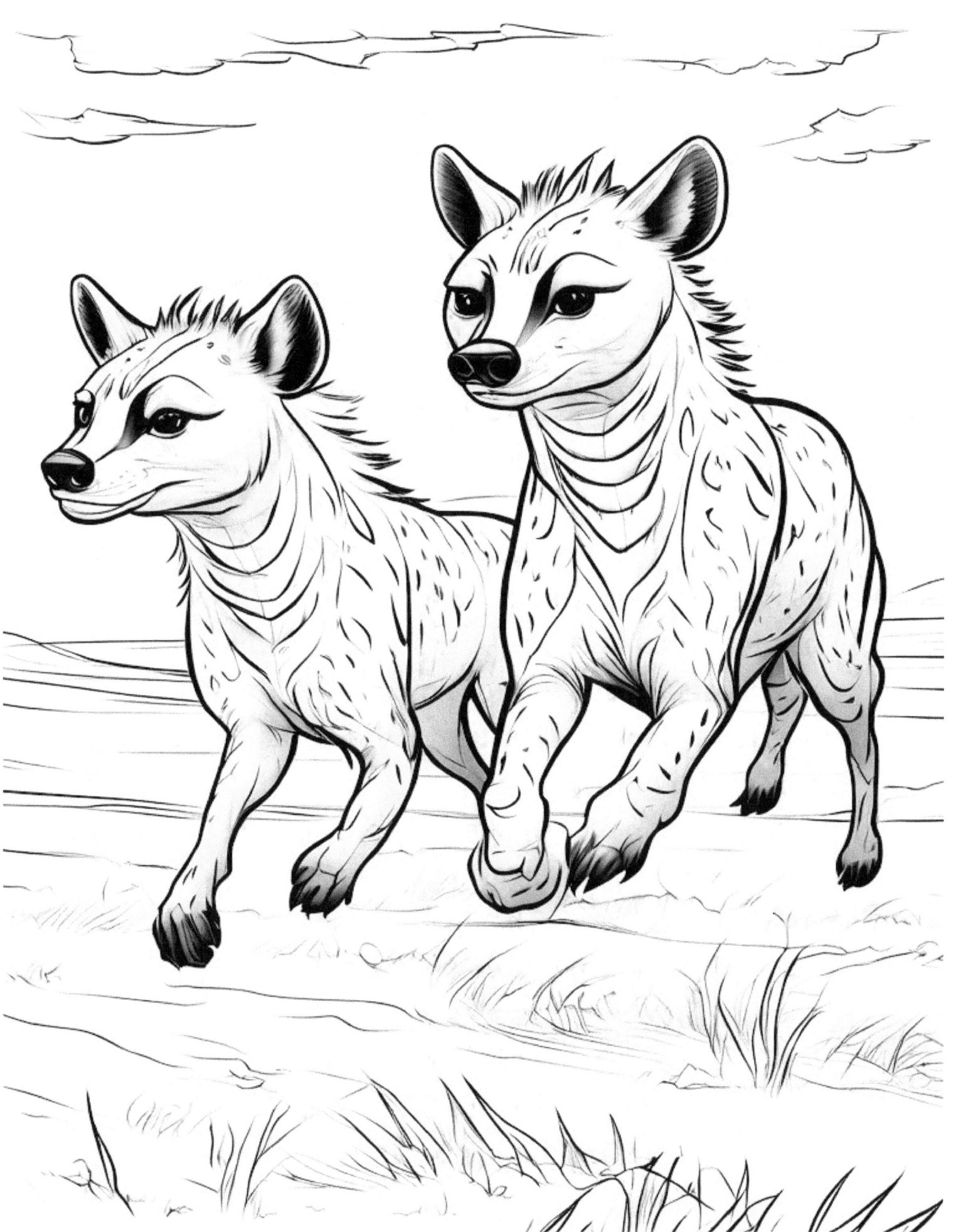

TIGER

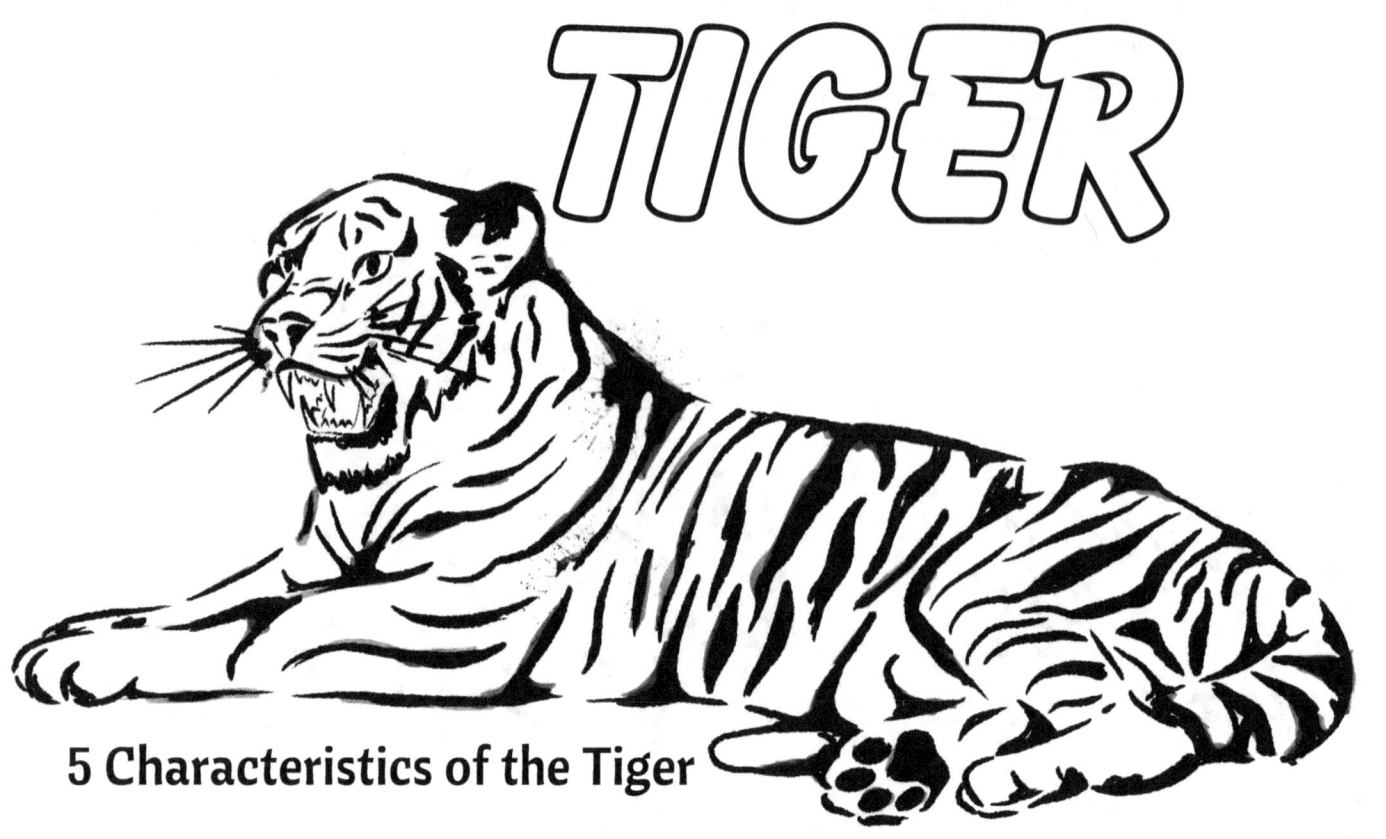

5 Characteristics of the Tiger

1. Is the largest feline in the world – The tiger is the largest and heaviest of all felines, weighing up to 660 lbs.
2. Has unique stripes – The tiger's stripes are like fingerprints, unique to each animal.
3. Is a great swimmer – The tiger loves swimming and can easily cross wide rivers.
4. Is a solitary hunter – Unlike other felines, the tiger hunts alone and is very strategic in its hunts.
5. Has a powerful bite – The tiger has an extremely strong bite, capable of bringing down large prey.

Which of these characteristics did you like learning about the most?
Write the number here: _____

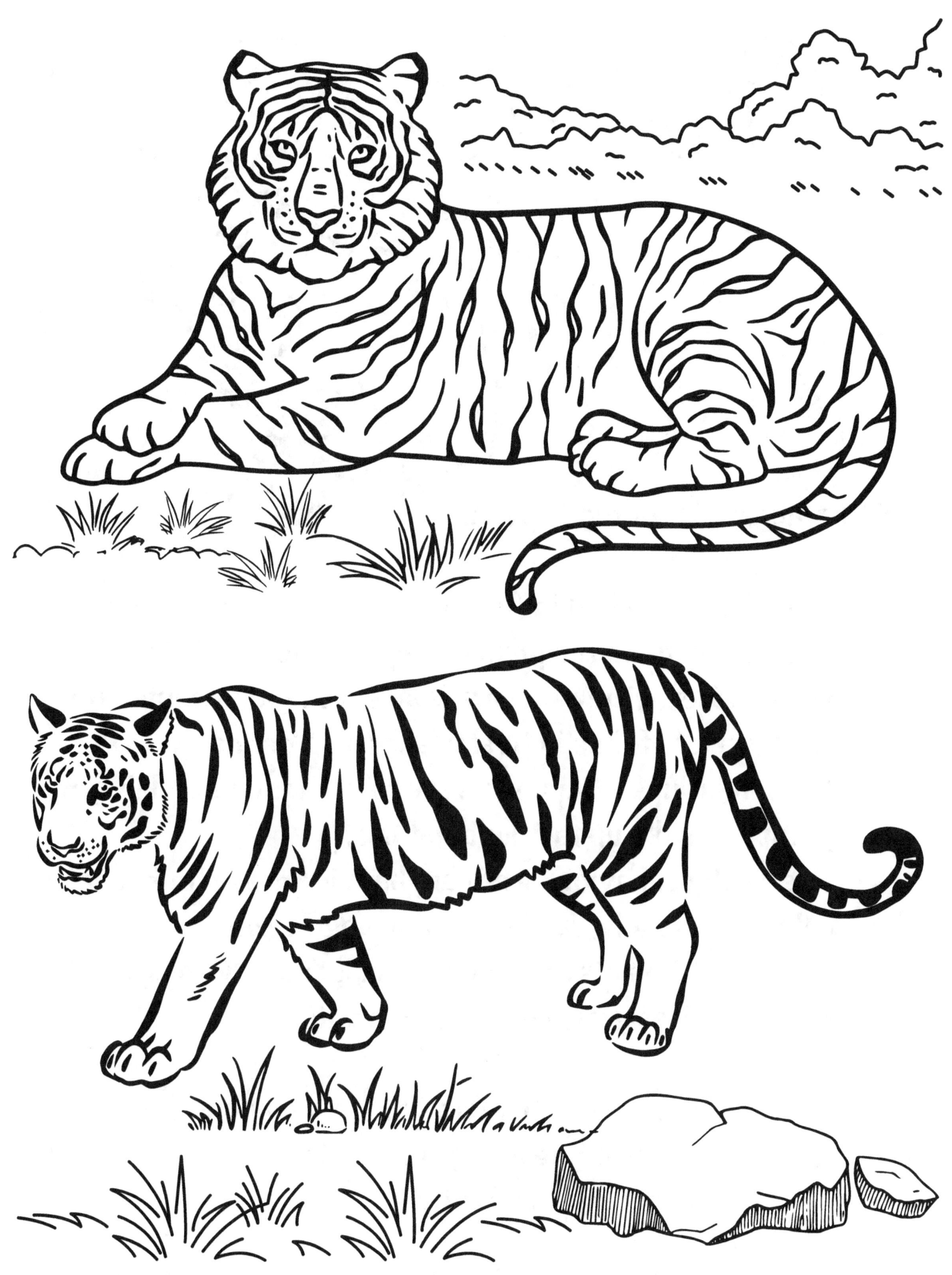

CAPYBARA

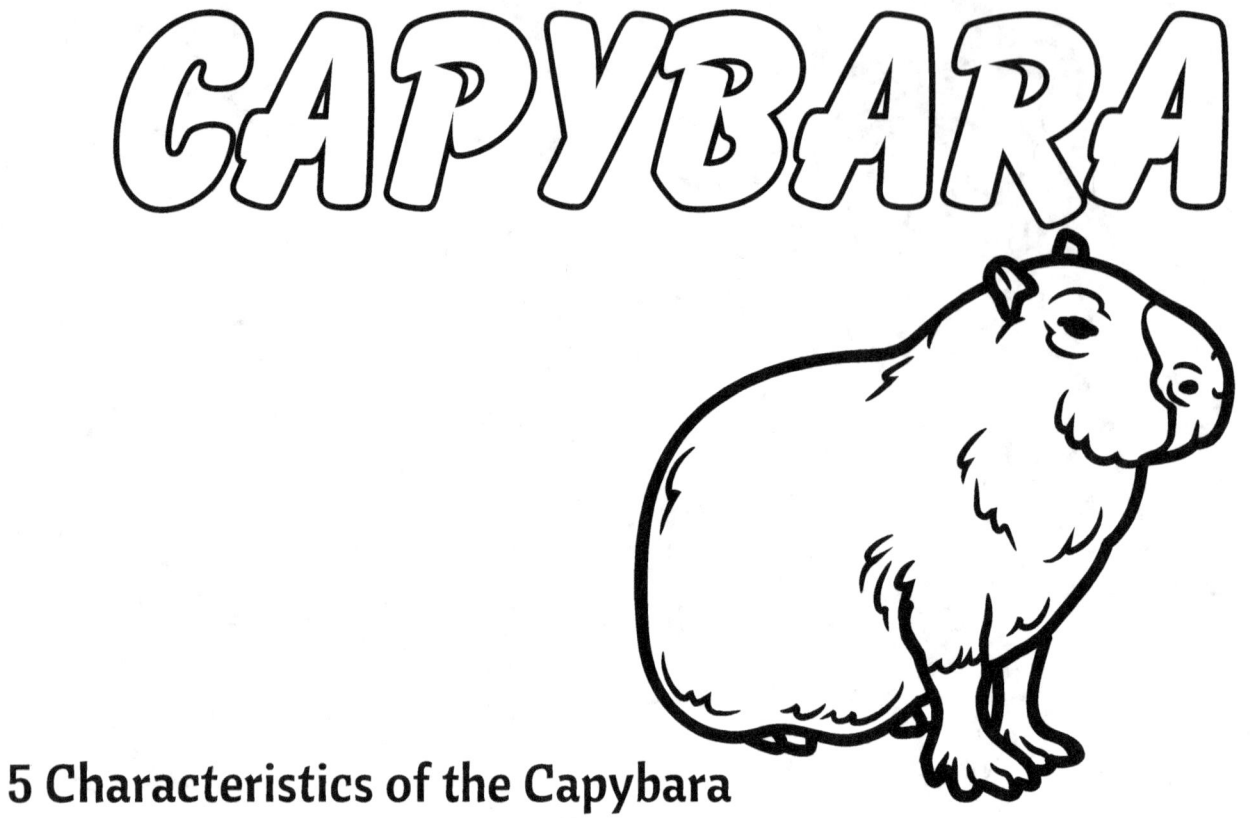

5 Characteristics of the Capybara

1. Is the largest rodent in the world – The capybara is the largest rodent on the planet, weighing up to 145 lbs.
2. Loves water – The capybara is an excellent swimmer and spends a lot of time in rivers, lakes, and ponds.
3. Lives in groups – Capybaras are social animals and live in groups, usually up to 20 individuals.
4. Has a calm behavior – The capybara is known for being calm and friendly, rarely showing aggression.
5. Eats aquatic plants and grass – Its diet mainly consists of plants, such as grass and aquatic plants.

Which of these characteristics did you like learning about the most?
Write the number here: _____

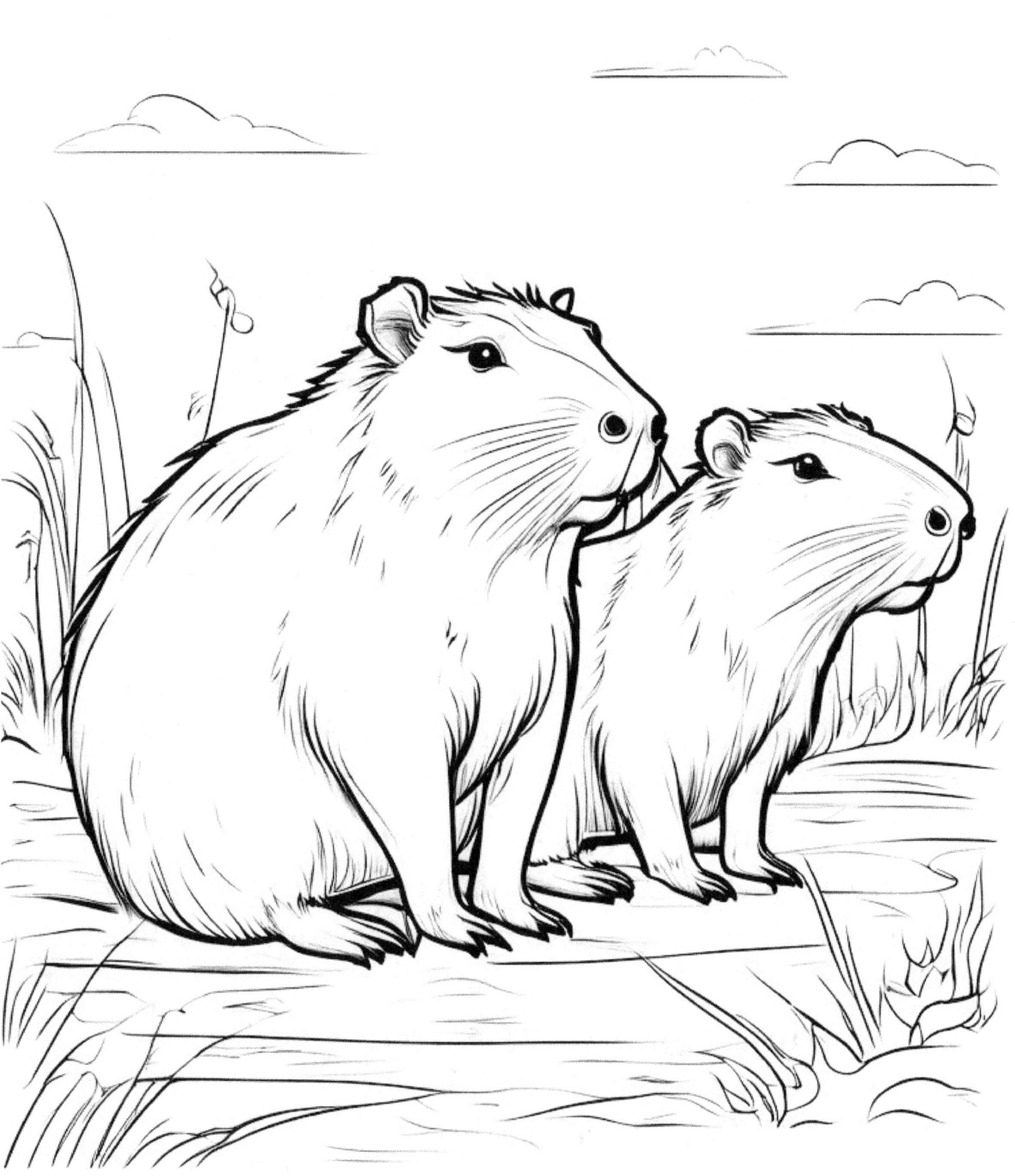

ELEPHANT

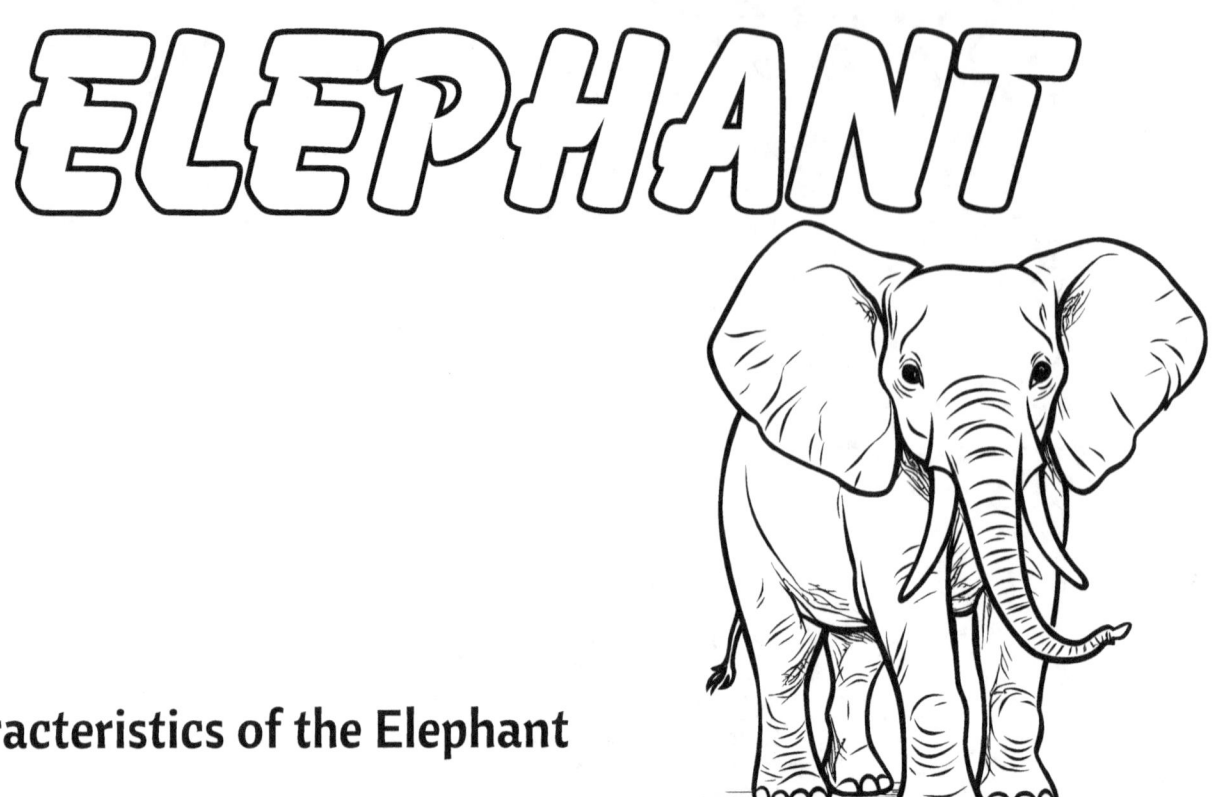

5 Characteristics of the Elephant

1. Is the largest land animal – The elephant is the largest land animal, weighing up to 13,000 lbs.
2. Has an amazing trunk – Its trunk is used for breathing, drinking water, picking up food, and even communicating.
3. Has ivory tusks – Elephants have long tusks, which are actually incisors, used for digging and searching for food.
4. Is a very social animal – Elephants live in groups called herds, with a complex social structure.
5. Is very intelligent – Elephants have great memory and can solve problems, use tools, and even show emotions.

Which of these characteristics did you like learning about the most?
Write the number here: _____

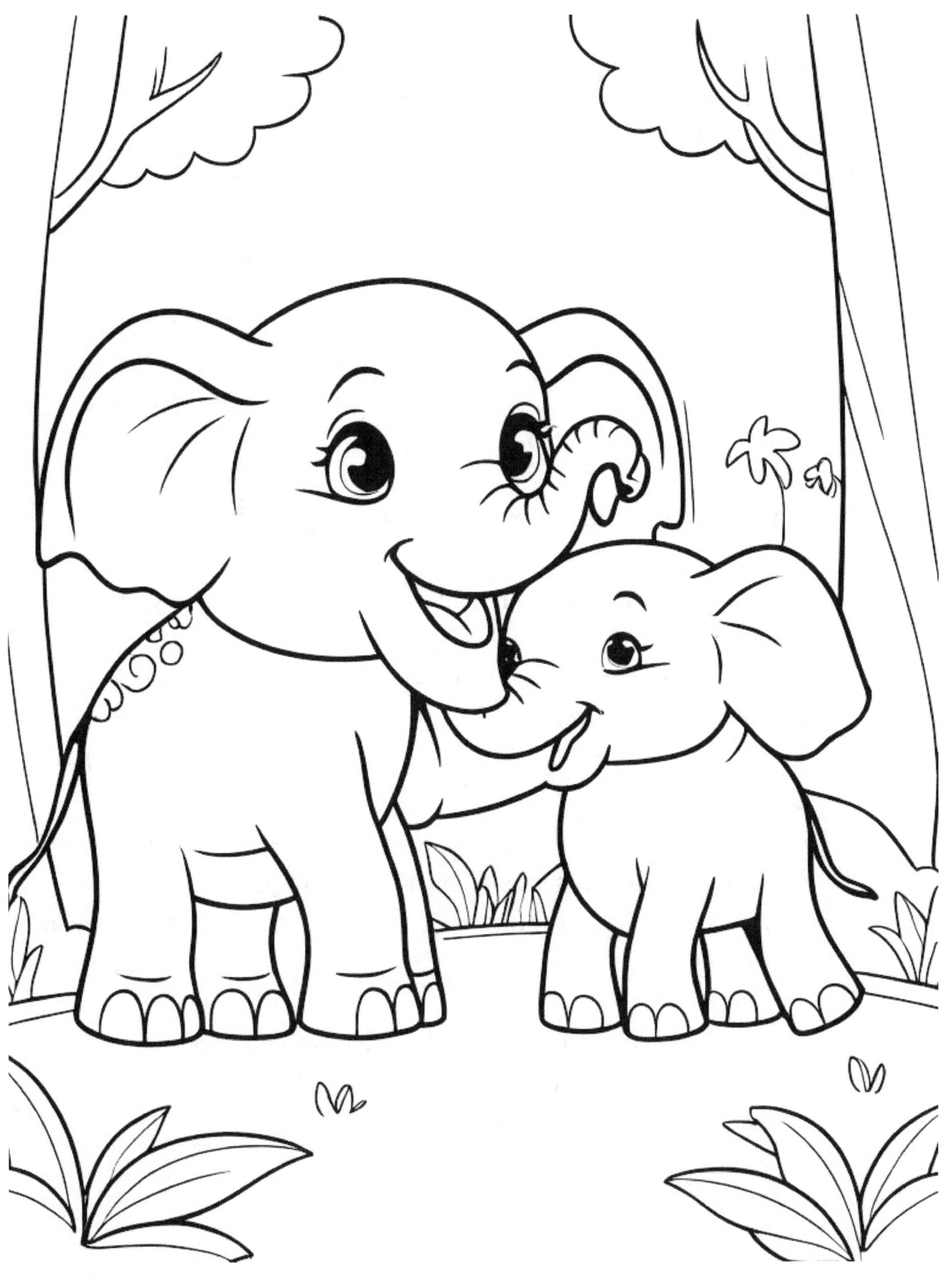

MONKEY

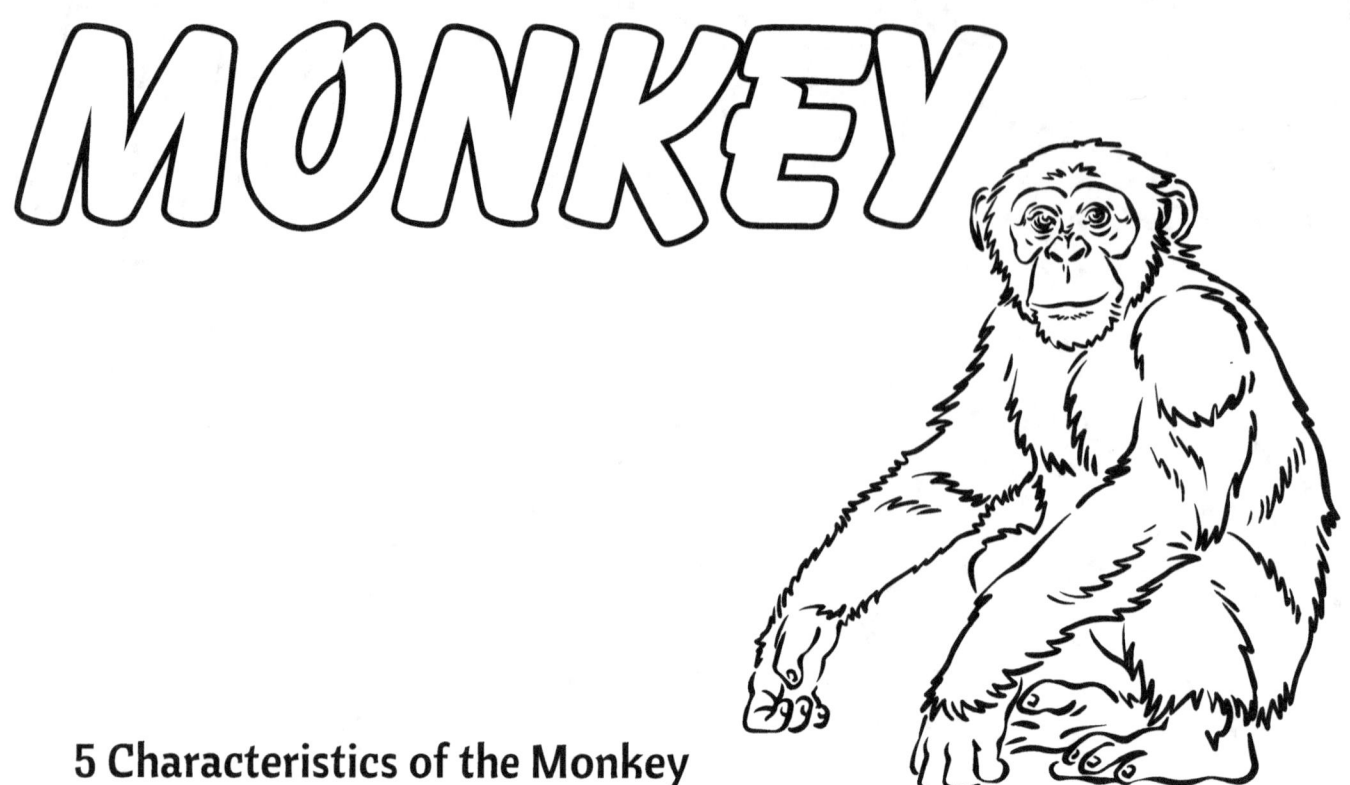

5 Characteristics of the Monkey

1. Is very agile – Monkeys are excellent climbers and move quickly through trees.
2. Uses hands to grab food – Monkeys have very skillful hands, allowing them to pick up and manipulate objects and food.
3. Are social animals – They live in groups, communicate, and help each other.
4. Are curious – Monkeys are very curious and love exploring their environment, always investigating new things.
5. Have a varied diet – Monkeys eat fruits, seeds, insects, and even small prey.

Which of these characteristics did you like learning about the most?
Write the number here: _____

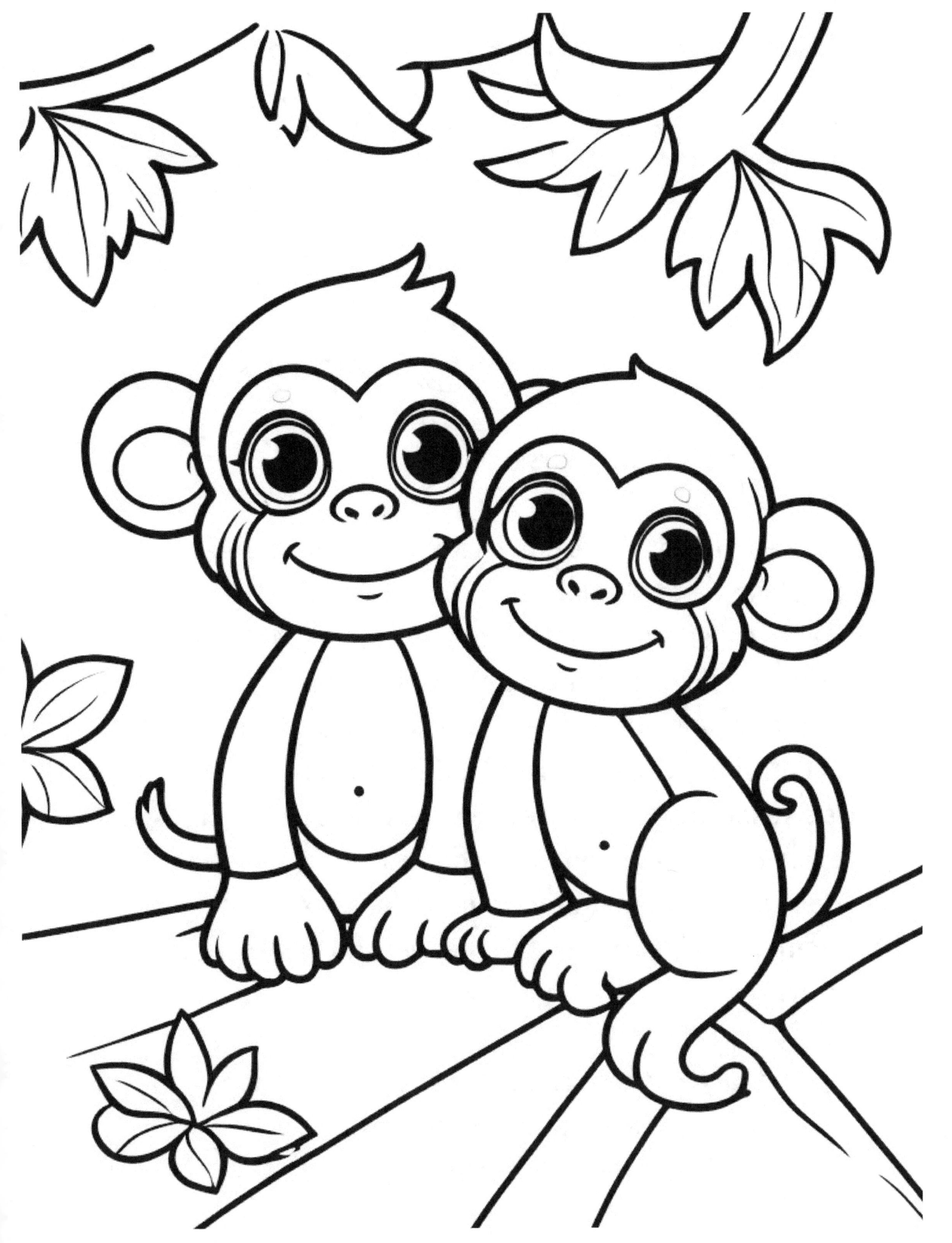

HORSE

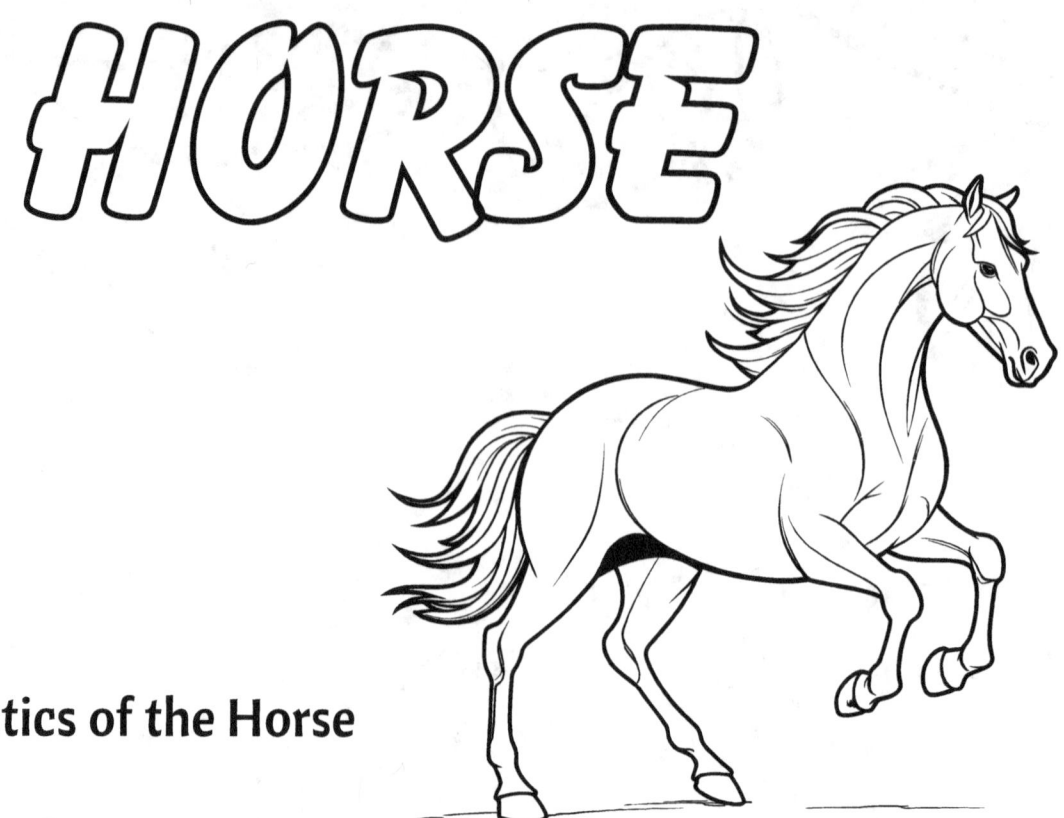

5 Characteristics of the Horse

1. Is a fast animal – The horse can run at great speeds, reaching up to 43 mph.
2. Has excellent vision – Horses have almost 360-degree vision, which helps them detect predators.
3. Is very strong – Horses are very strong animals, capable of carrying heavy loads and pulling carts.
4. Is a social animal – Horses live in groups called herds and enjoy interacting with other horses.
5. Has impressive memory – Horses have excellent memory and can remember people and places for many years.

Which of these characteristics did you like learning about the most?
Write the number here: _____

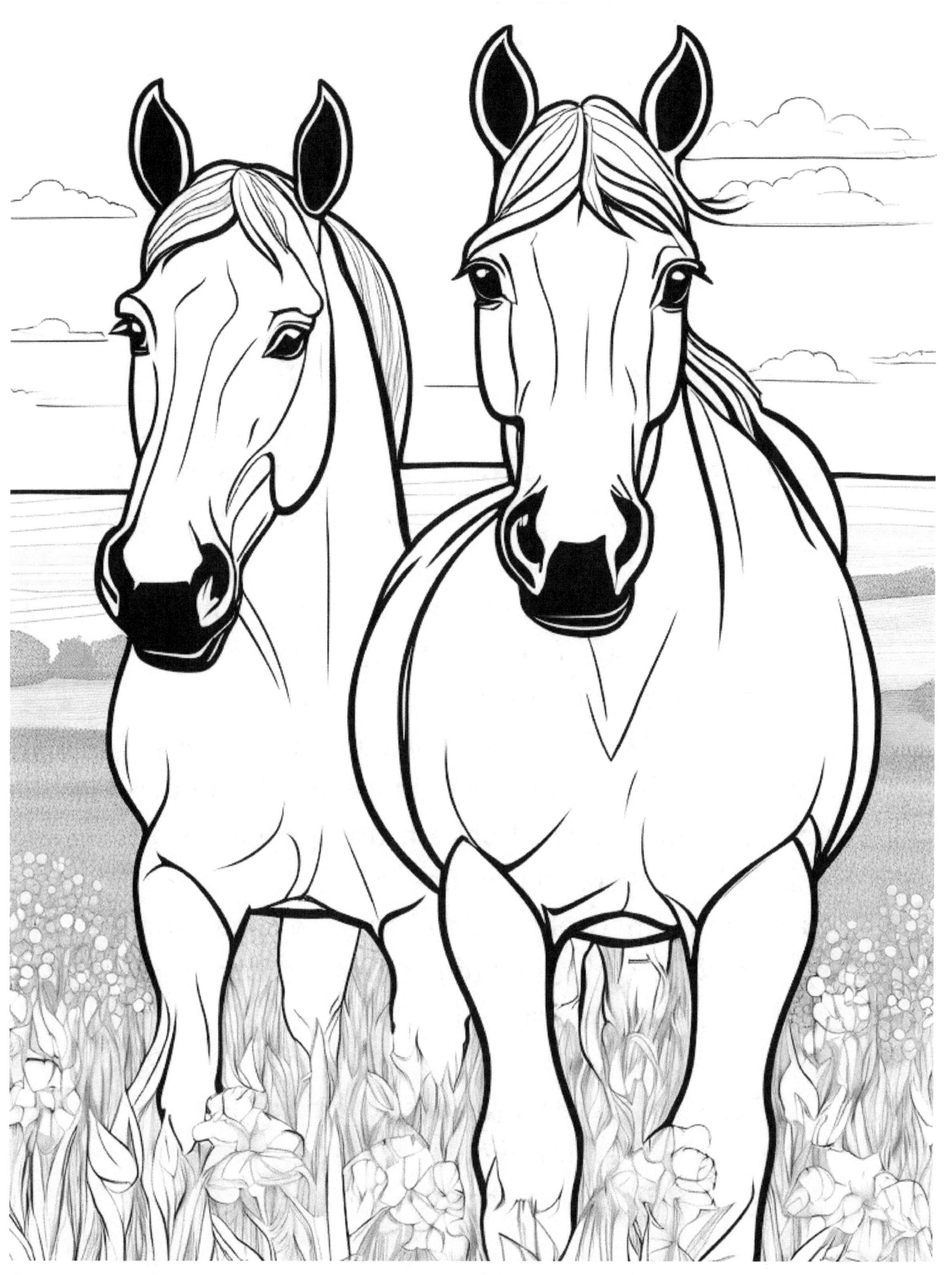

DOG

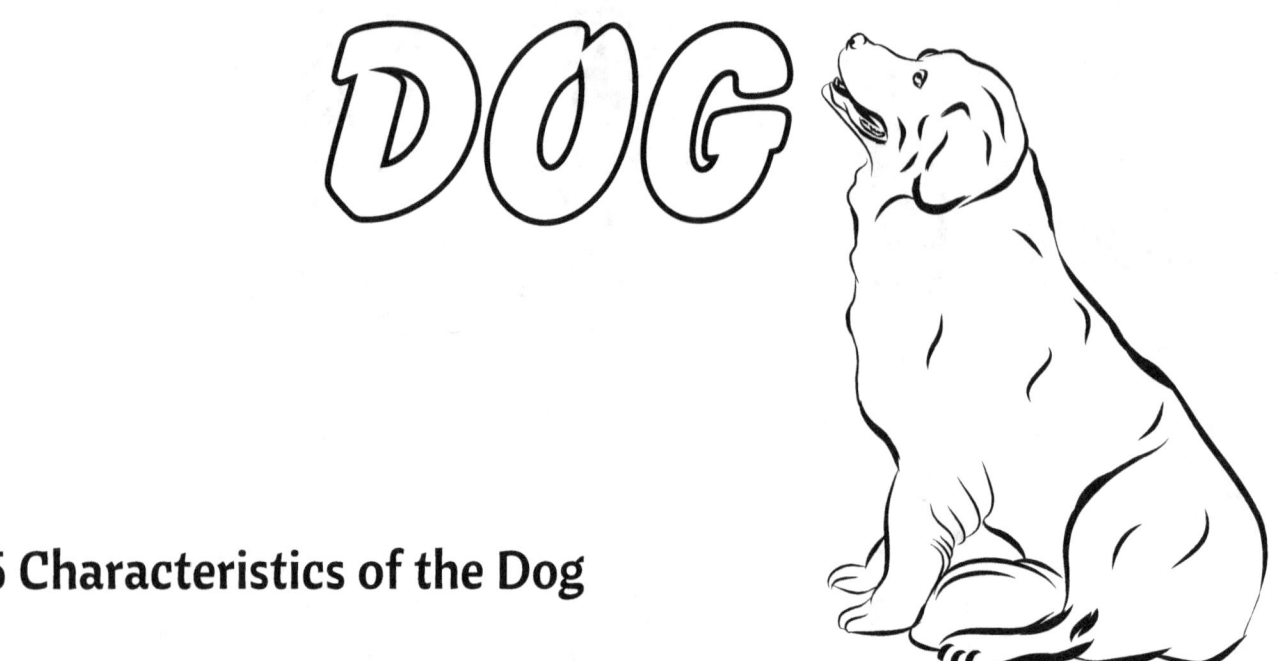

5 Characteristics of the Dog

1. Is a great friend – Dogs are known for being loyal and always accompanying their owners, making them great friends.
2. Has an amazing sense of smell – Dogs have a much better sense of smell than humans, capable of detecting scents from long distances.
3. Is very sociable – Dogs love being around people and other animals, and are very friendly and affectionate.
4. Can be trained easily – Dogs are intelligent and can quickly learn tricks and commands.
5. Has a wide variety of breeds – There are many different types of dogs, each with unique characteristics such as size, coat, and temperament.

Which of these characteristics did you like learning about the most?
Write the number here: _____

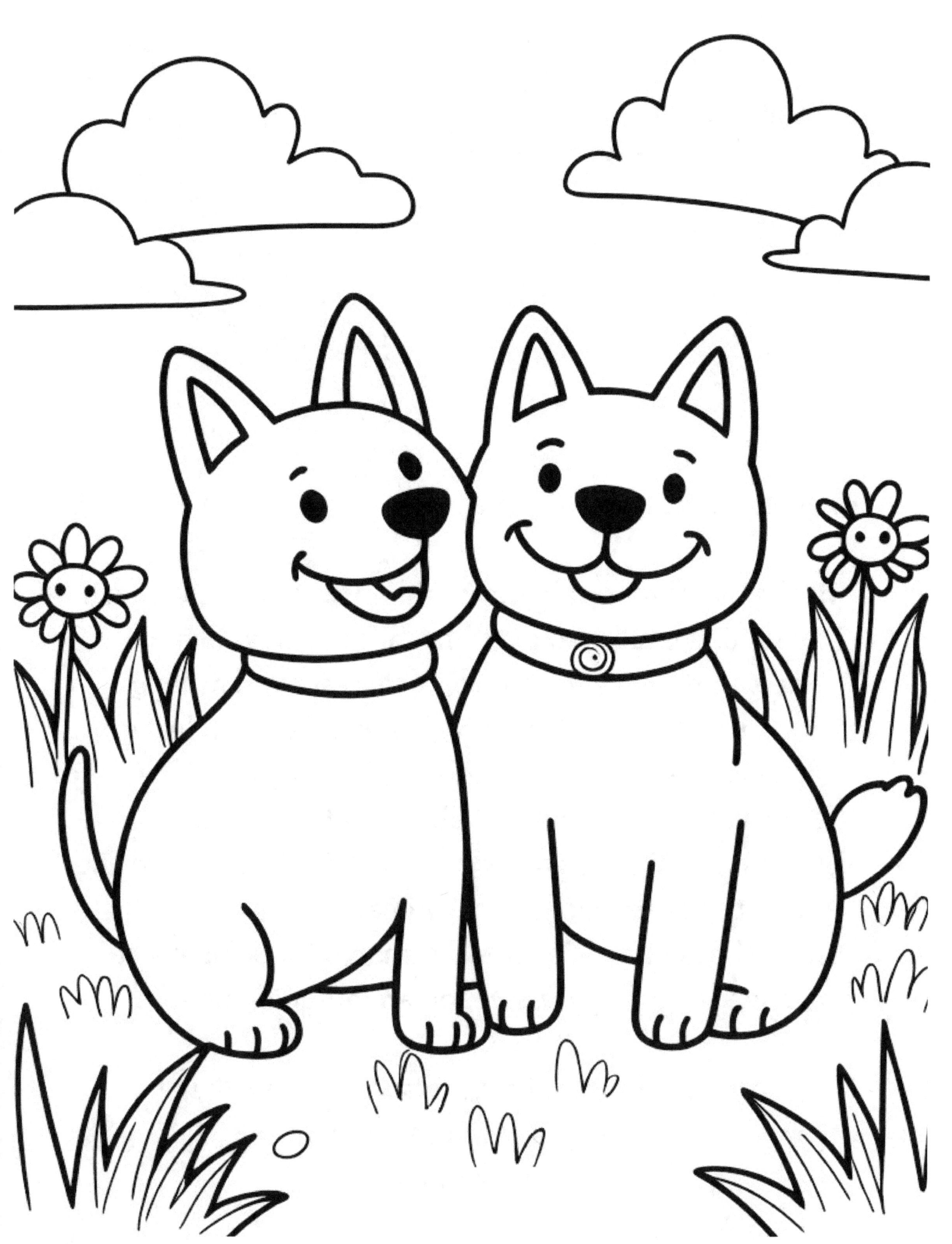

GIRAFFE

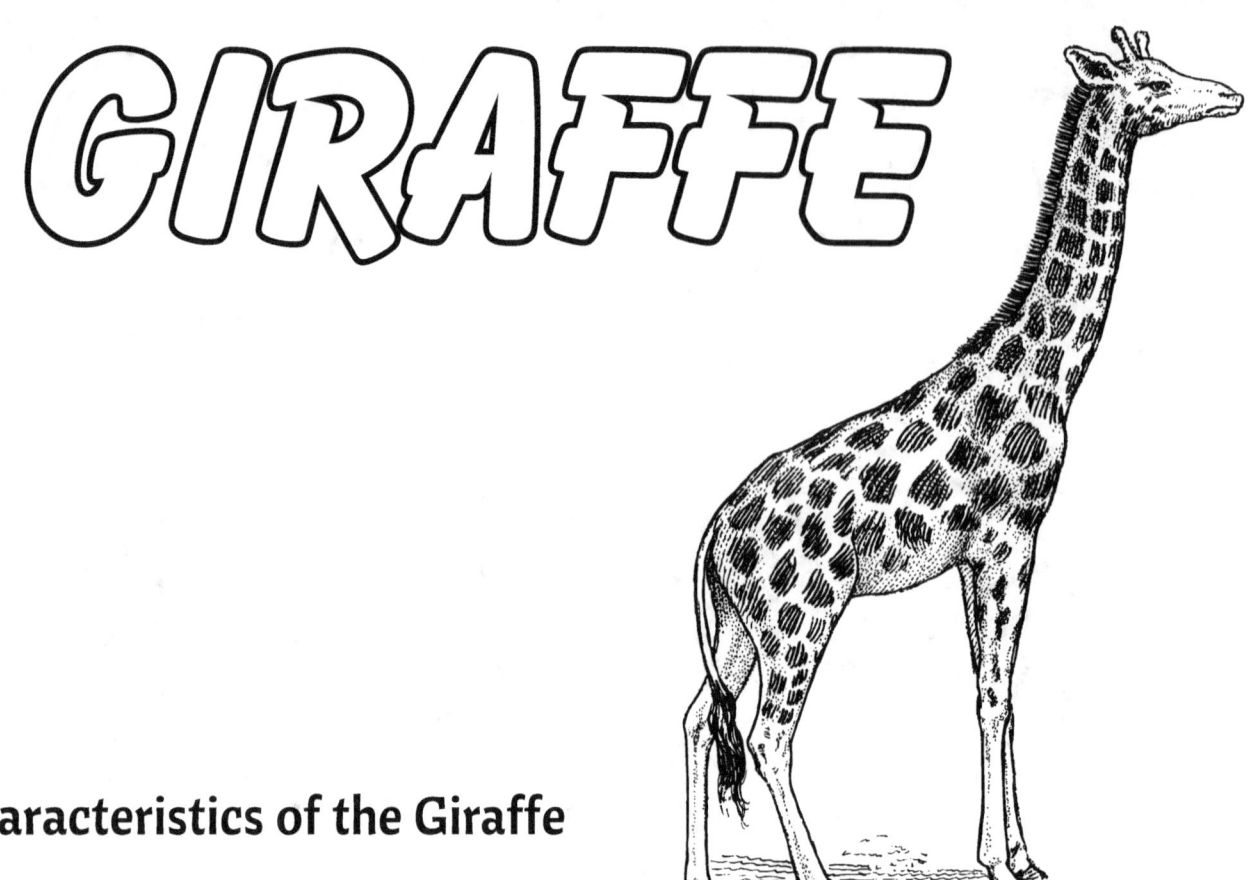

5 Characteristics of the Giraffe

1. Is the tallest animal in the world – The giraffe can reach up to 18 feet tall, making it the tallest land animal.
2. Has a long neck – Its most notable feature is its long neck, which helps it reach high branches to eat leaves.
3. Its tongue is very long – The giraffe's tongue can be up to 18 inches long, helping it grab leaves from trees.
4. Has unique spots on its skin – The giraffe's spots are like fingerprints, unique to each animal.
5. Is a calm animal – Giraffes are known for being peaceful and usually not aggressive toward other animals.

Which of these characteristics did you like learning about the most?
Write the number here: _____

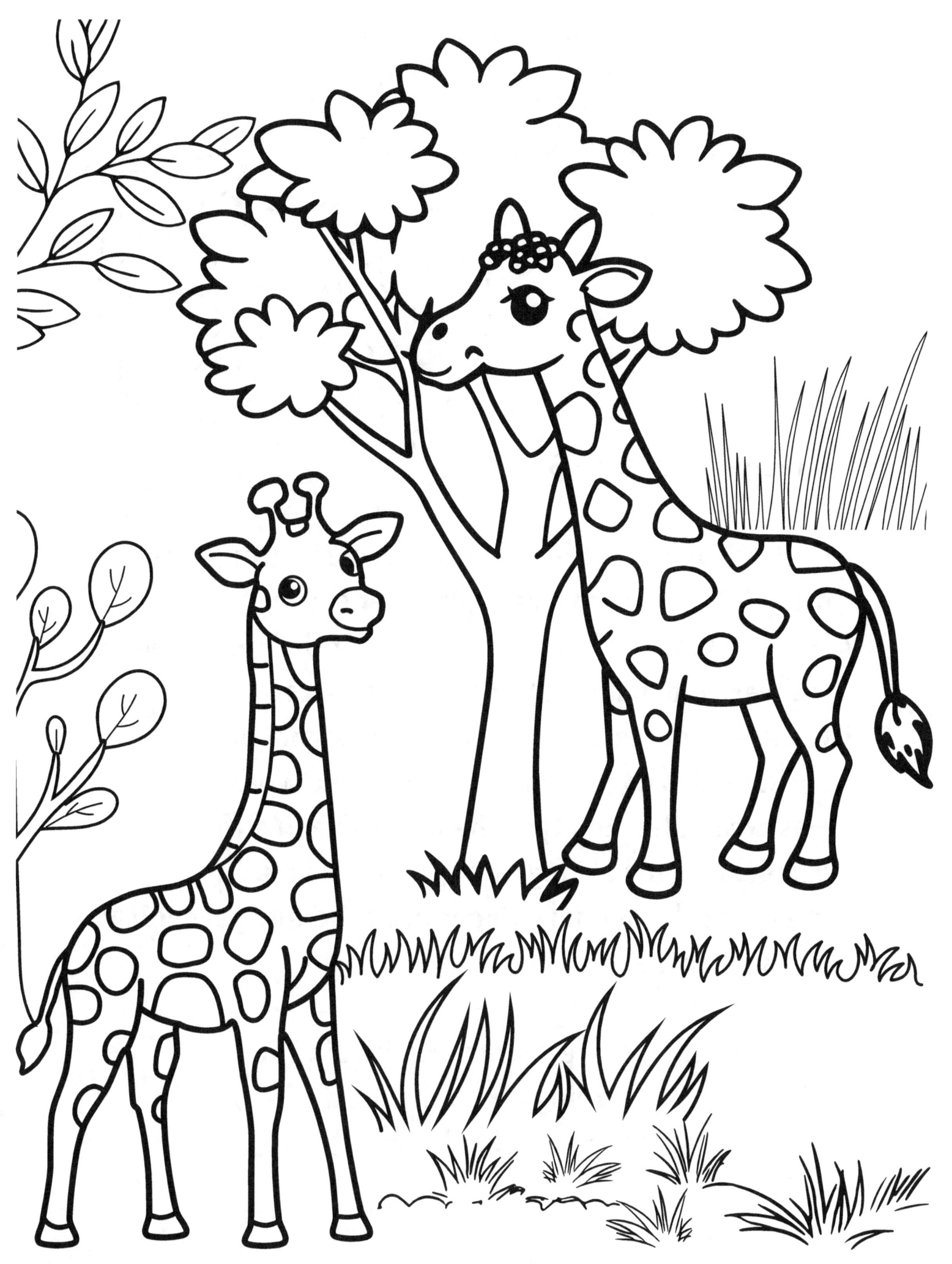

SHEEP

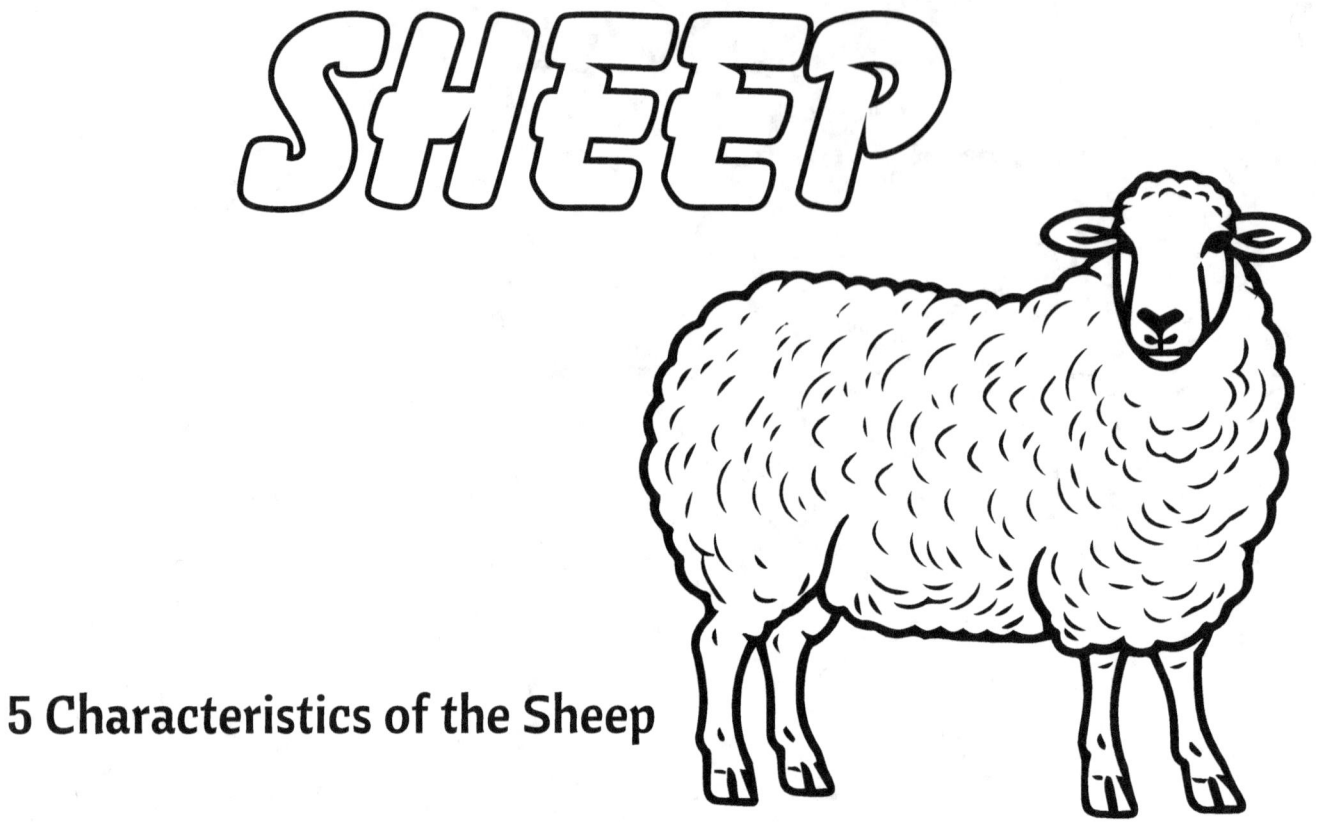

5 Characteristics of the Sheep

1. Is a herd animal – Sheep prefer to live in groups and often follow the leadership of other sheep.
2. Has soft wool – Sheep are famous for their wool, which is sheared to make clothing and blankets.
3. Is a great source of food – Sheep meat and milk are consumed in many cultures around the world.
4. Has great adaptability – Sheep can live in different climates, from cold regions to warmer areas.
5. Is a very calm animal – Sheep are generally peaceful and not aggressive.

Which of these characteristics did you like learning about the most?
Write the number here: _____

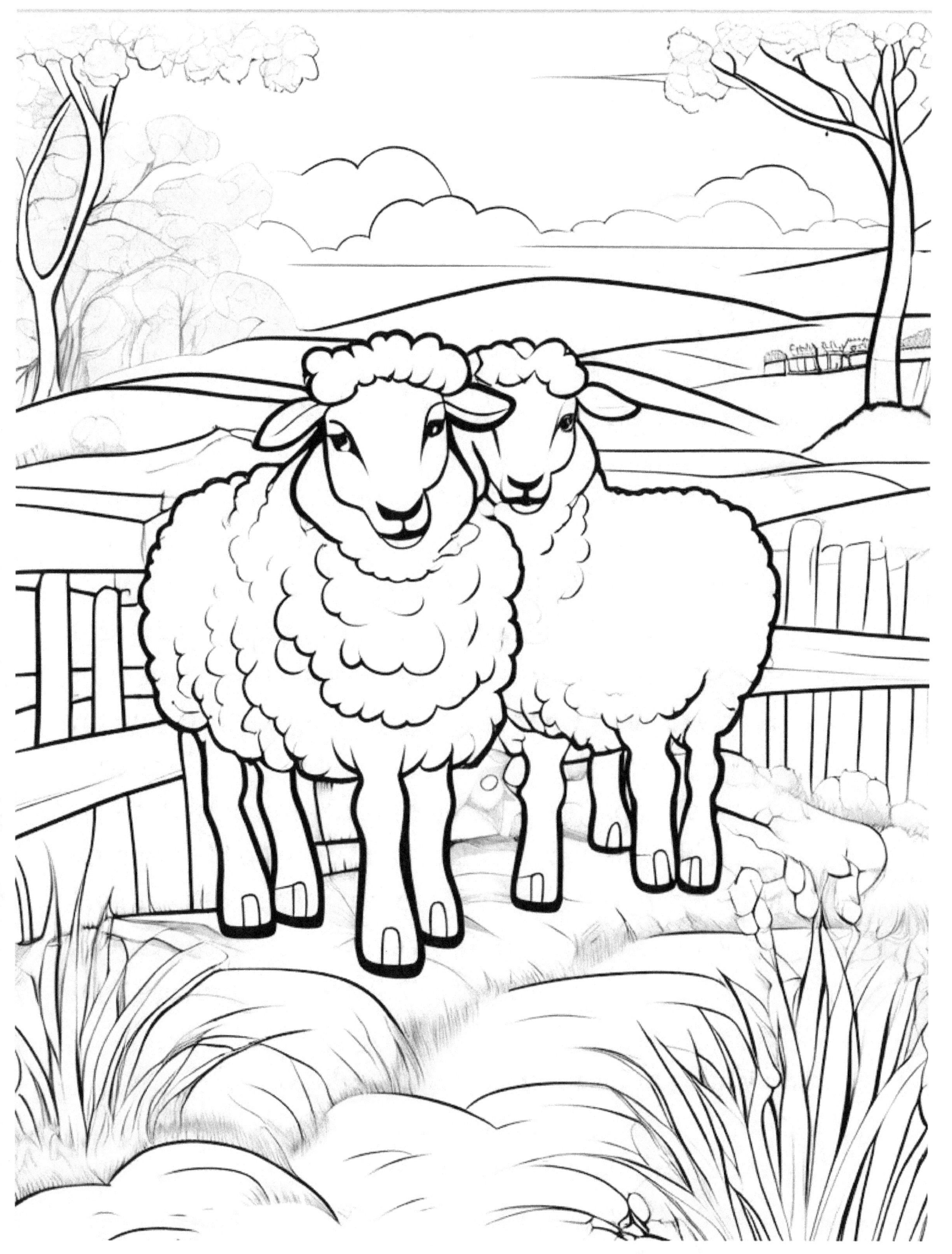

SLOTH ANIMAL

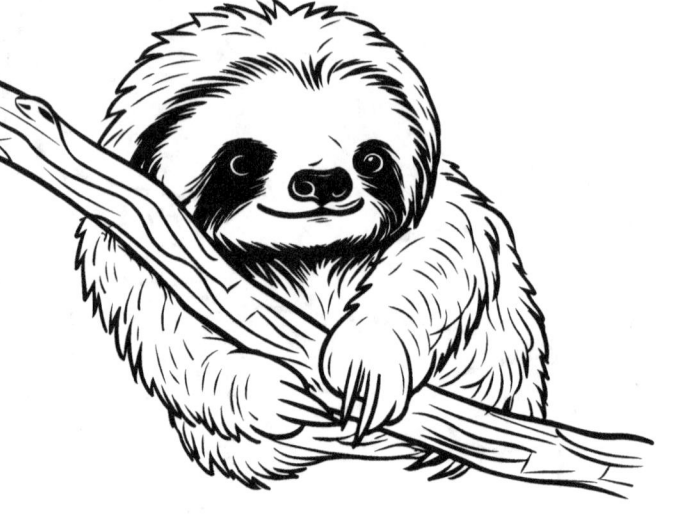

5 Characteristics of the Sloth

1. Is one of the slowest animals – The sloth is known for its slowness, moving at a speed of only 0.03 mph.
2. Spends most of its time sleeping – It can sleep up to 20 hours a day, mostly hanging from trees.
3. Is great at climbing trees – Despite its slowness, the sloth is an excellent climber, using its long claws to cling to branches.
4. Has a simple diet – Its diet mainly consists of leaves, which are hard to digest and provide little energy.
5. Has an extremely slow metabolism – The sloth has such a slow metabolism that its digestive system can take up to a whole week to process food.

Which of these characteristics did you like learning about the most?
Write the number here: _____

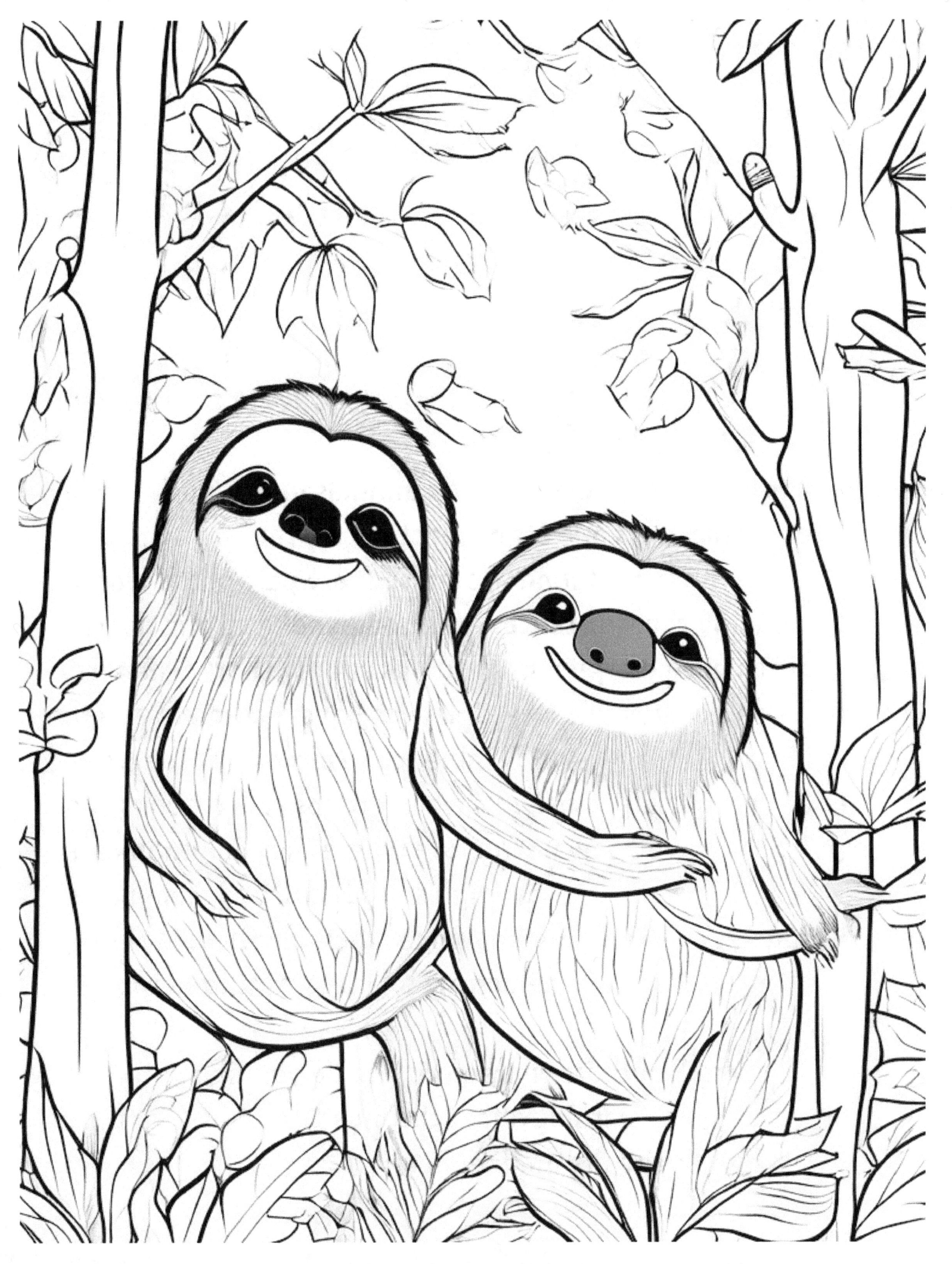

CHICKEN

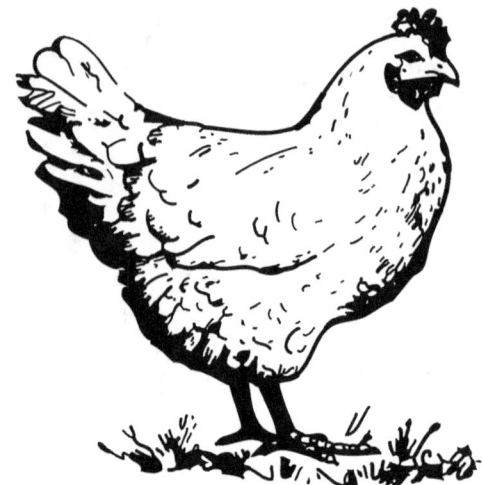
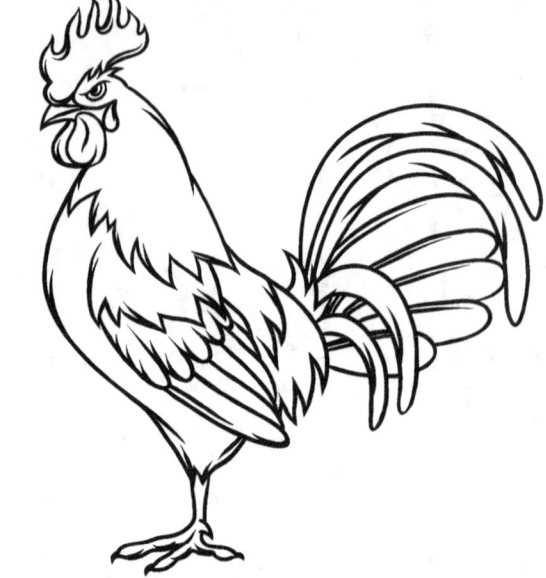

5 Characteristics of the Chicken

1. Is one of the most common animals in the world – The chicken is one of the most widely raised animals by humans, found in almost every part of the world.
2. Can fly short distances – Although not a strong flyer, a chicken can give small jumps and fly short distances.
3. Has excellent vision – Chickens have incredible vision, able to see almost 360 degrees.
4. Is very social – Chickens live in groups called flocks and have a social structure where they communicate through sounds and body language.
5. Lays eggs – Hens are known for their ability to lay eggs, which are an important food source.

Which of these characteristics did you like learning about the most?
Write the number here: _____

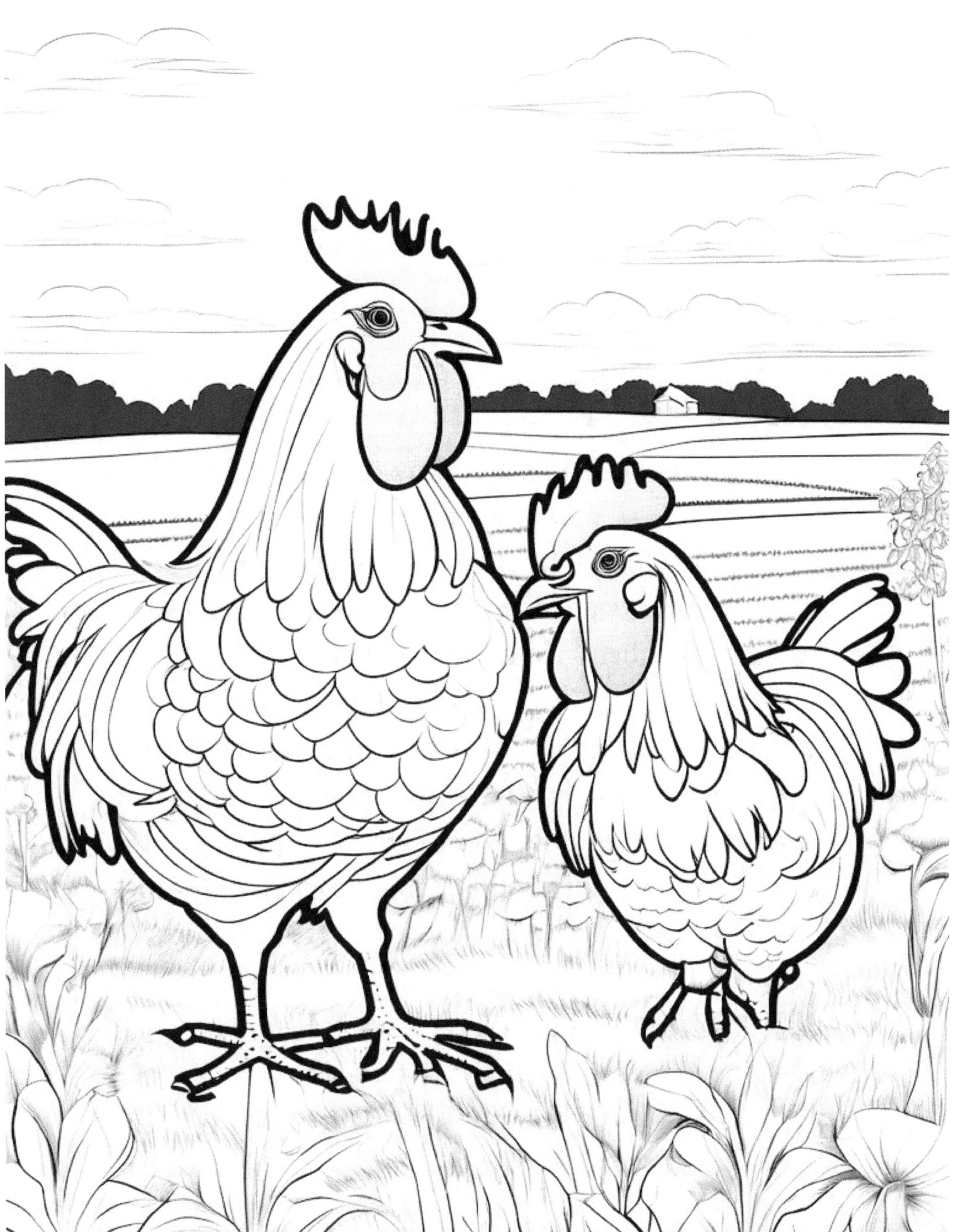

GOAT

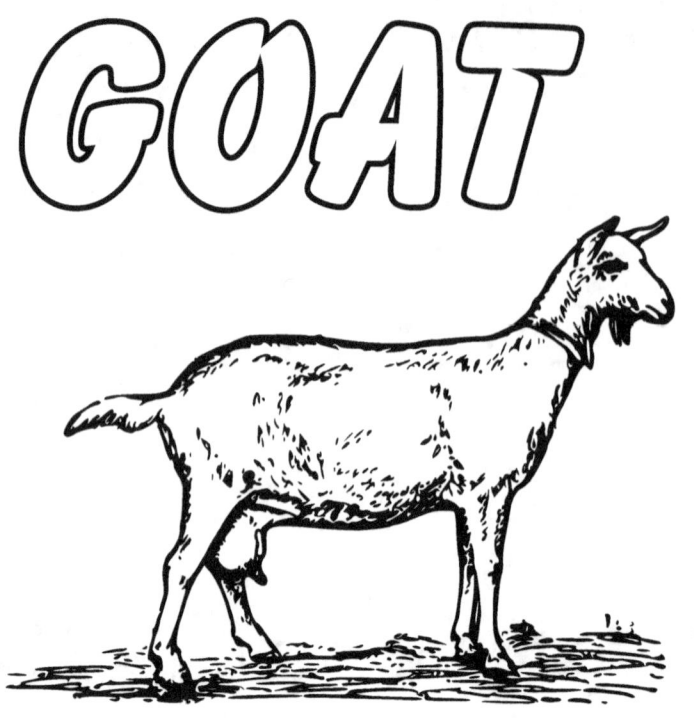
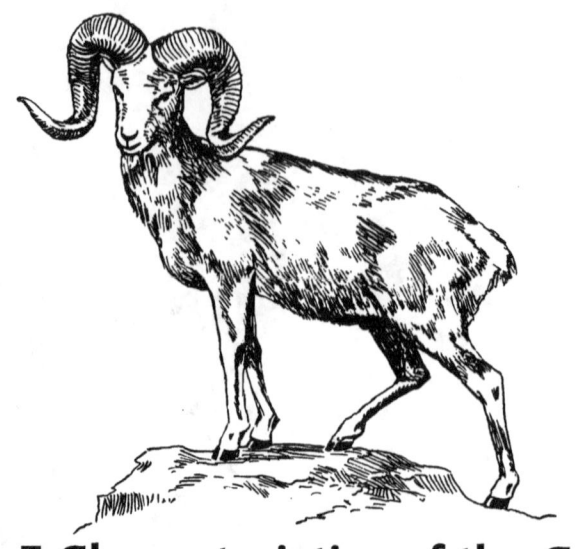

5 Characteristics of the Goat

1. Is very curious – Goats are known for being very curious and love exploring their surroundings.
2. Likes to climb – Goats are excellent climbers and can easily scale steep mountains and rocky surfaces.
3. Has a varied diet – Goats eat almost anything, including plants, bushes, and even wood!
4. Has a keen sense of smell – Goats have a very good sense of smell, which helps them find food and detect danger.
5. Is an excellent jumper – Goats can jump long distances, which helps them escape predators and explore new areas.

Which of these characteristics did you like learning about the most?
Write the number here: _____

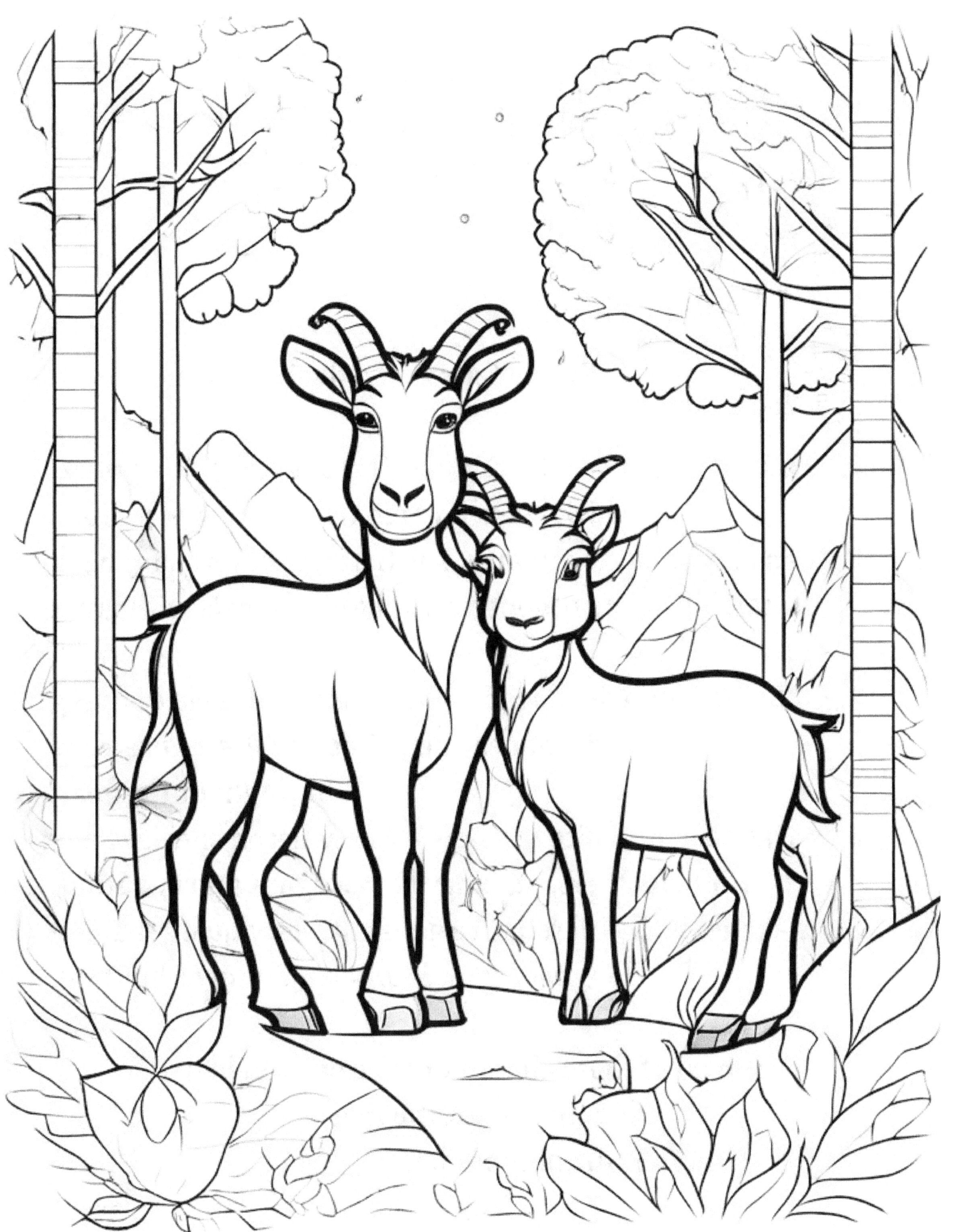

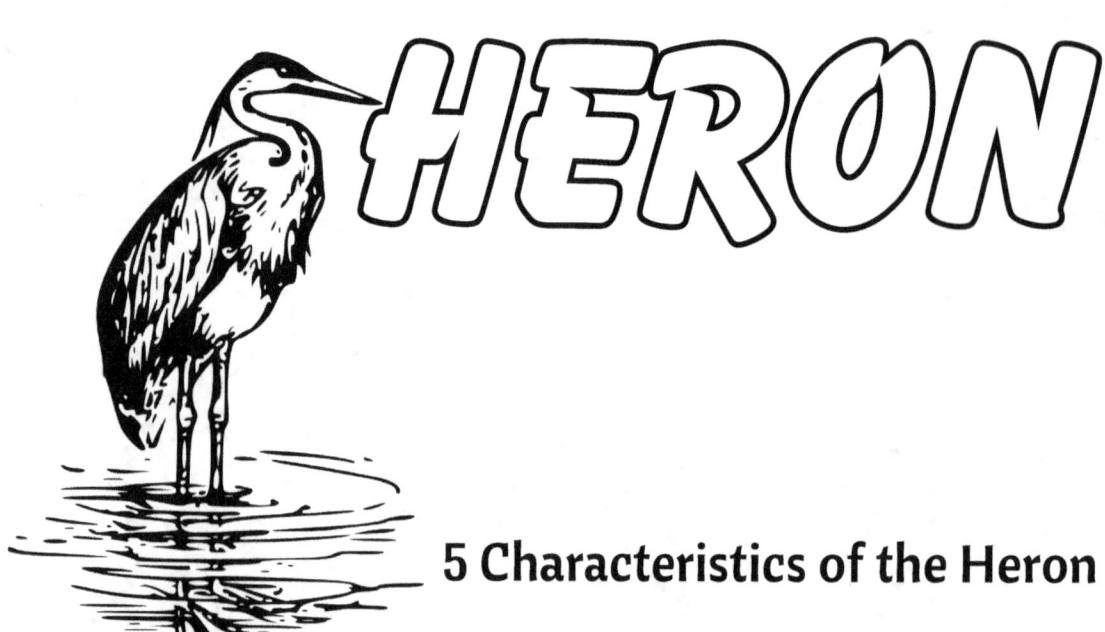

5 Characteristics of the Heron

1. Has a long neck – The heron is famous for its long neck, which helps it catch fish in shallow waters.
2. Is an excellent fisherman – The heron uses its sharp beak to catch fish and other small aquatic animals with great skill.
3. Can fly long distances – The heron is capable of flying great distances, migrating to different regions throughout the year.
4. Has elegant white feathers – Many heron species have white feathers, making them elegant and beautiful.
5. Is a quiet bird – Herons are generally very quiet, making few sounds while moving or hunting.

Which of these characteristics did you like learning about the most?
Write the number here: _____

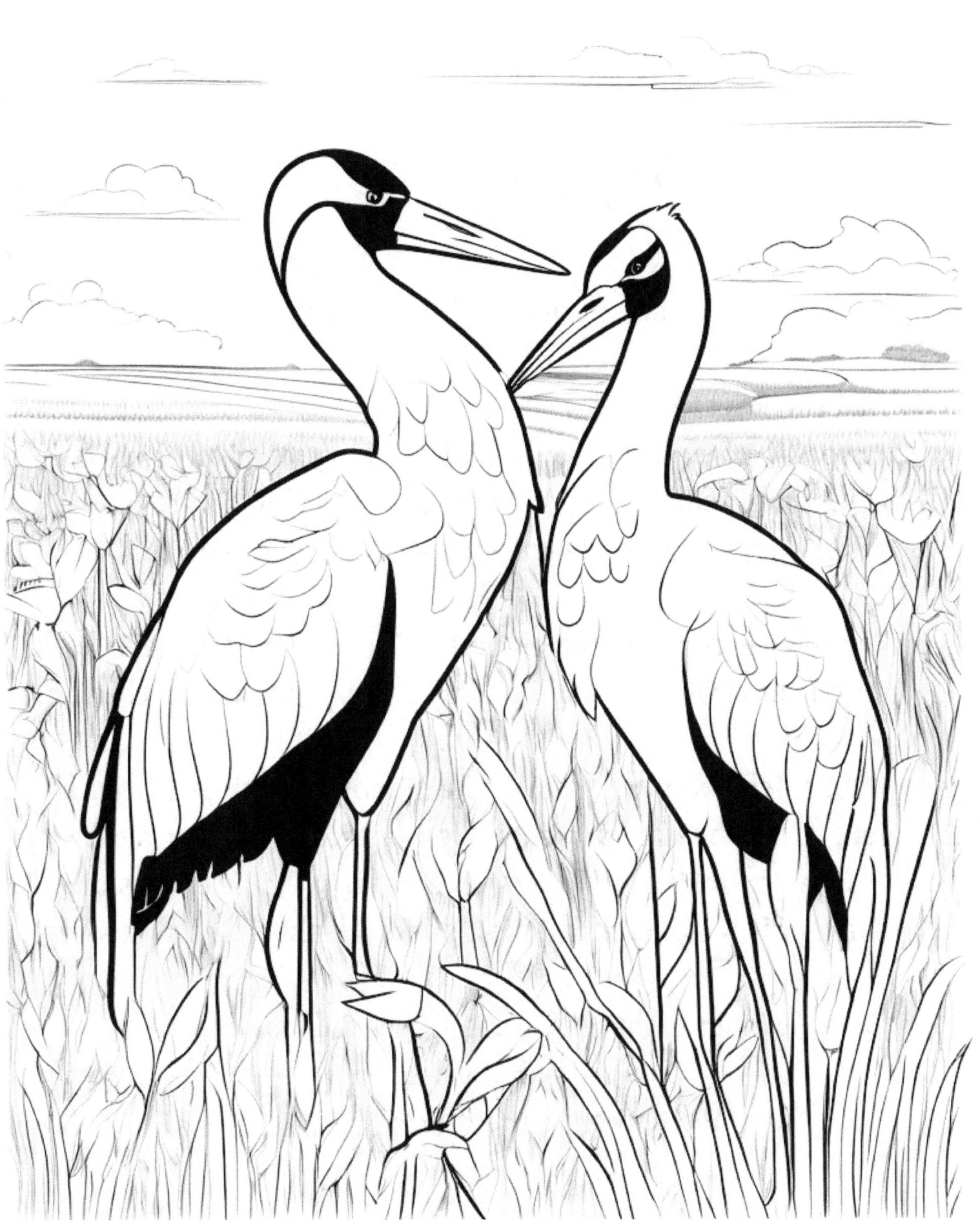

CROCODILE

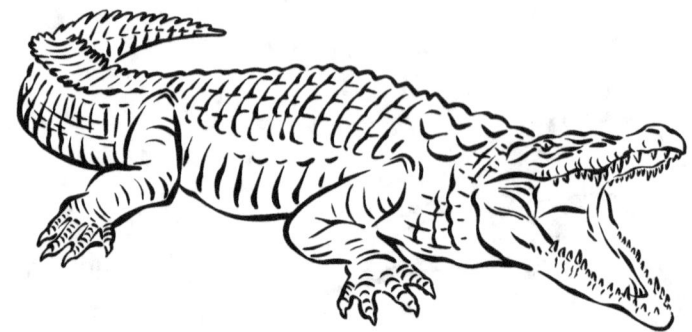

5 Characteristics of the Crocodile

1. Has a powerful jaw – The crocodile has a very strong jaw, capable of crushing bones and catching its prey with ease.
2. Is an excellent hunter – Crocodiles are highly efficient predators, using patience and camouflage to ambush their prey.
3. Lives both in water and on land – Crocodiles can live in both aquatic environments and on land, easily moving between the two.
4. Has thick and tough skin – The crocodile's skin is thick and very tough, helping protect it from attacks and even sunburn.
5. Can go for long periods without eating – Due to its slow metabolism, the crocodile can go for weeks without feeding.

Which of these characteristics did you like learning about the most?
Write the number here: _____

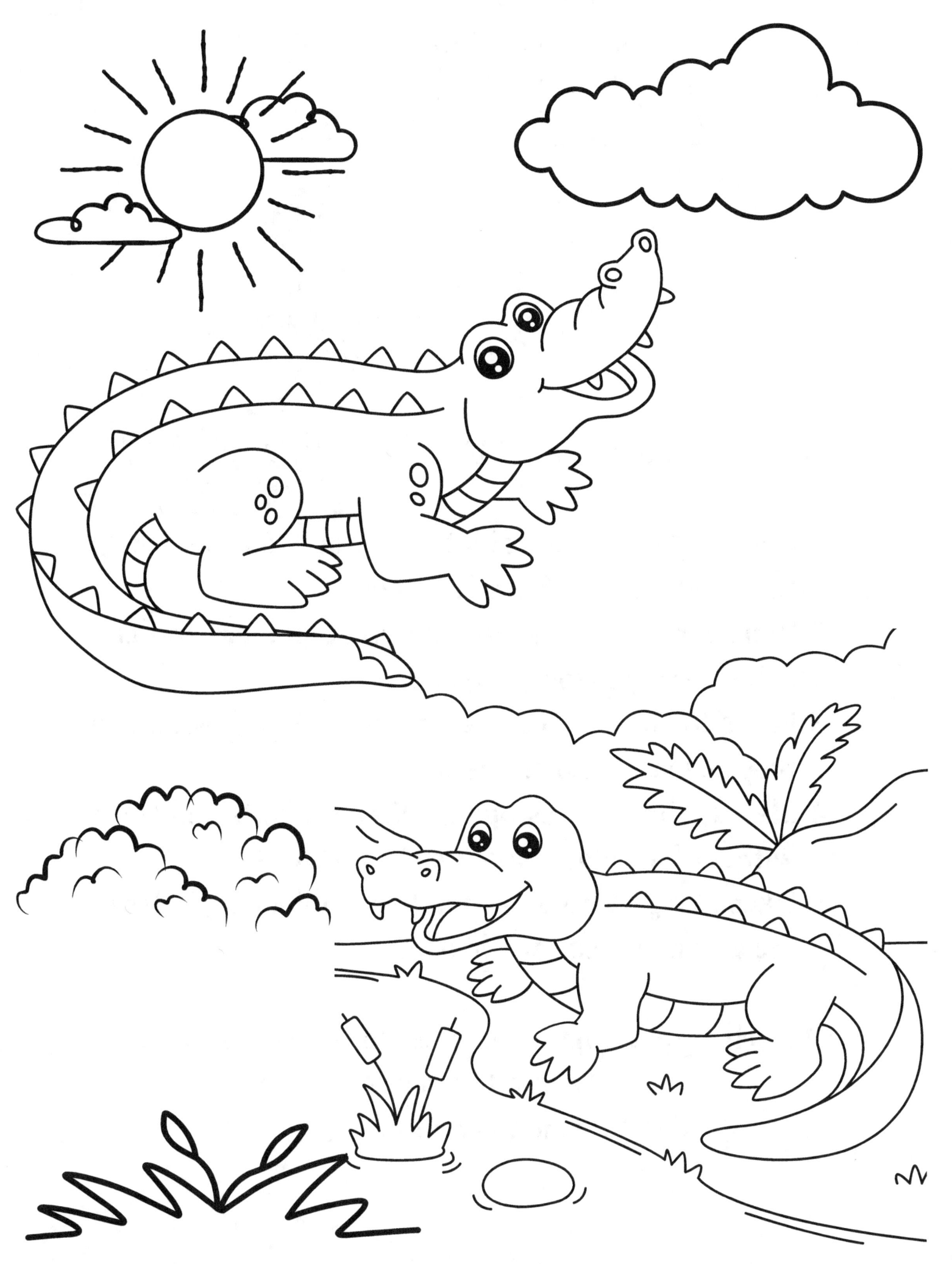

RABBIT

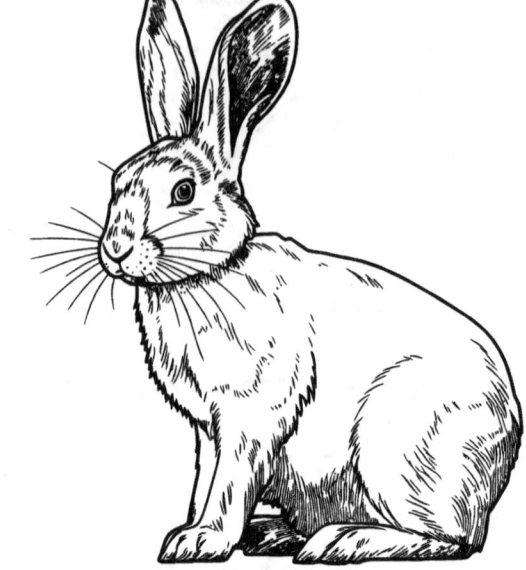

5 Characteristics of the Rabbit

1. Has long ears – A rabbit's ears are long and help them hear sounds from far away.
2. Runs very fast – Rabbits are great runners and can quickly escape from predators.
3. Loves to chew – Their teeth never stop growing, so they need to chew all the time.
4. Sleeps with its eyes open – Some rabbits can sleep without fully closing their eyes to stay alert.
5. Likes to dig burrows – In nature, rabbits dig holes in the ground to hide and live in.

Which of these characteristics did you like learning about the most?
Write the number here: _____

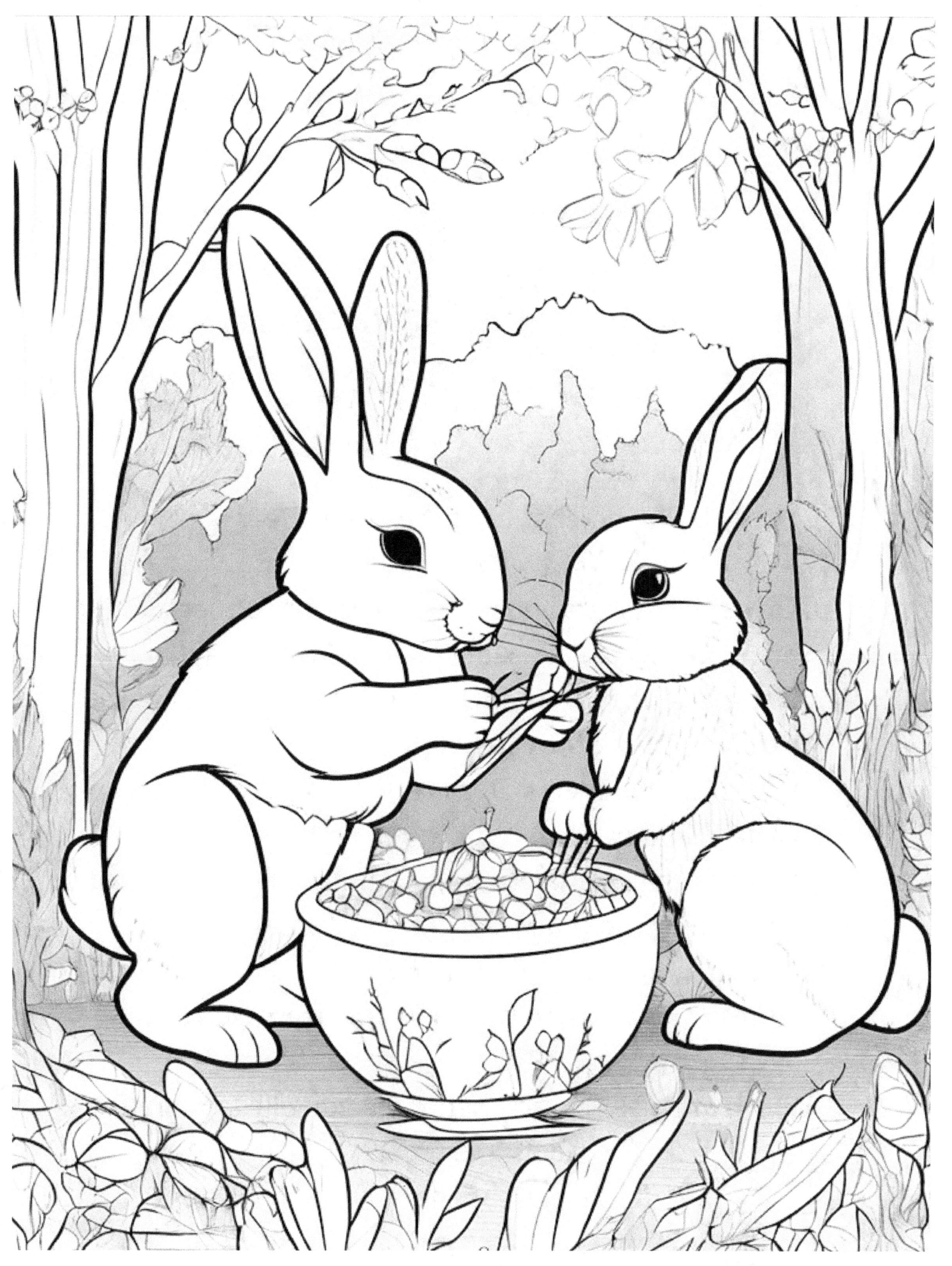

PANDA BEAR

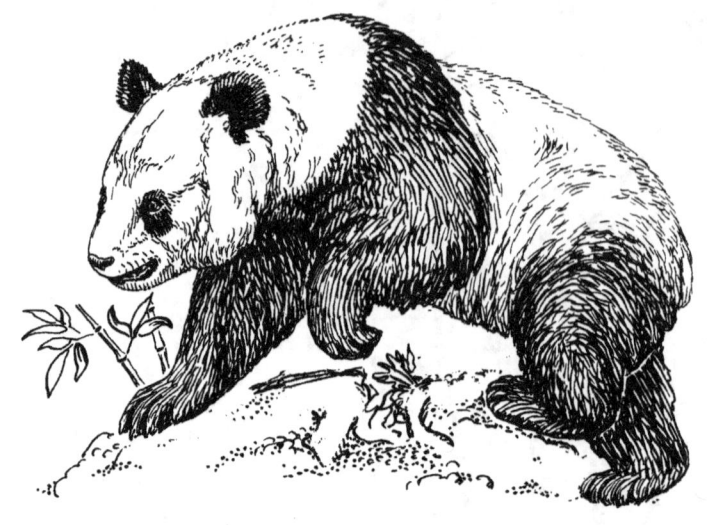

5 Characteristics of the Panda Bear

1. Loves to eat bamboo – Pandas eat almost only bamboo and can consume many kilos per day!
2. Has black and white fur – Their fluffy fur has black patches around the eyes, ears, and legs.
3. Is a great climber – Despite their size, pandas can easily climb trees.
4. Likes to roll on the ground – Pandas are playful and love rolling around in the grass and snow.
5. Has a funny way of walking – Pandas walk in a clumsy and amusing way, swaying from side to side.

Which of these characteristics did you like learning about the most?
Write the number here: _____

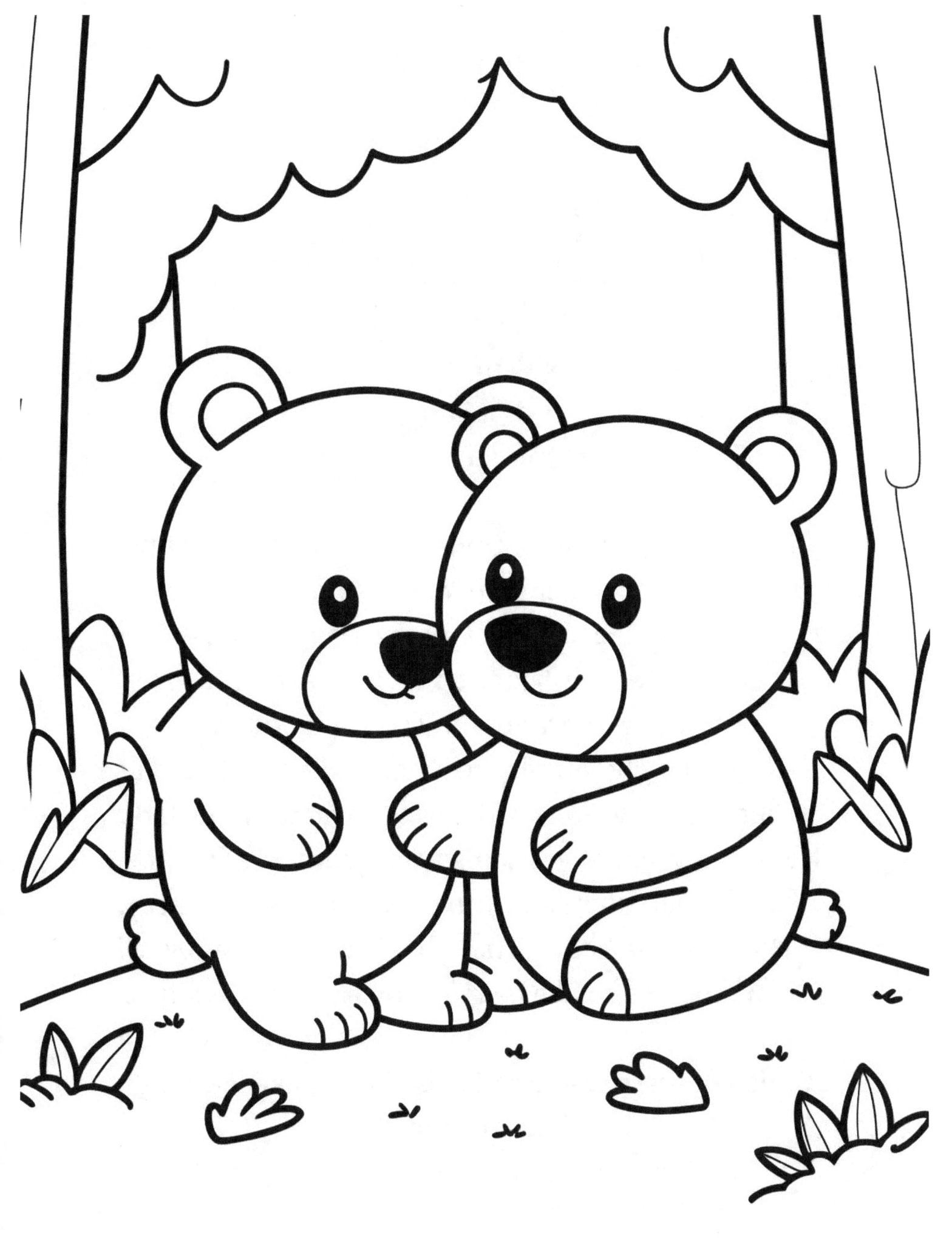

OWL

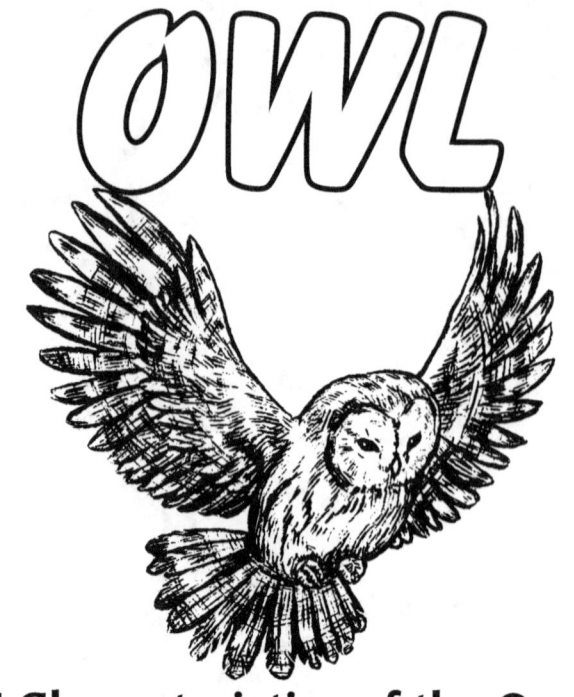

5 Characteristics of the Owl

1. Has big, bright eyes – Owls have huge eyes that help them see in the dark.
2. Can turn its head almost all the way around – They can rotate their heads up to 270 degrees to look around without moving their bodies.
3. Hunts at night – Owls are nocturnal animals and use their sharp vision and hearing to hunt in the dark.
4. Flies very quietly – Their special feathers allow them to fly without making noise, surprising their prey.
5. Has a unique hoot – The "hoo-hoo" sound of owls is famous and can be heard from far away in nature.

Which of these characteristics did you like learning about the most?
Write the number here: _____

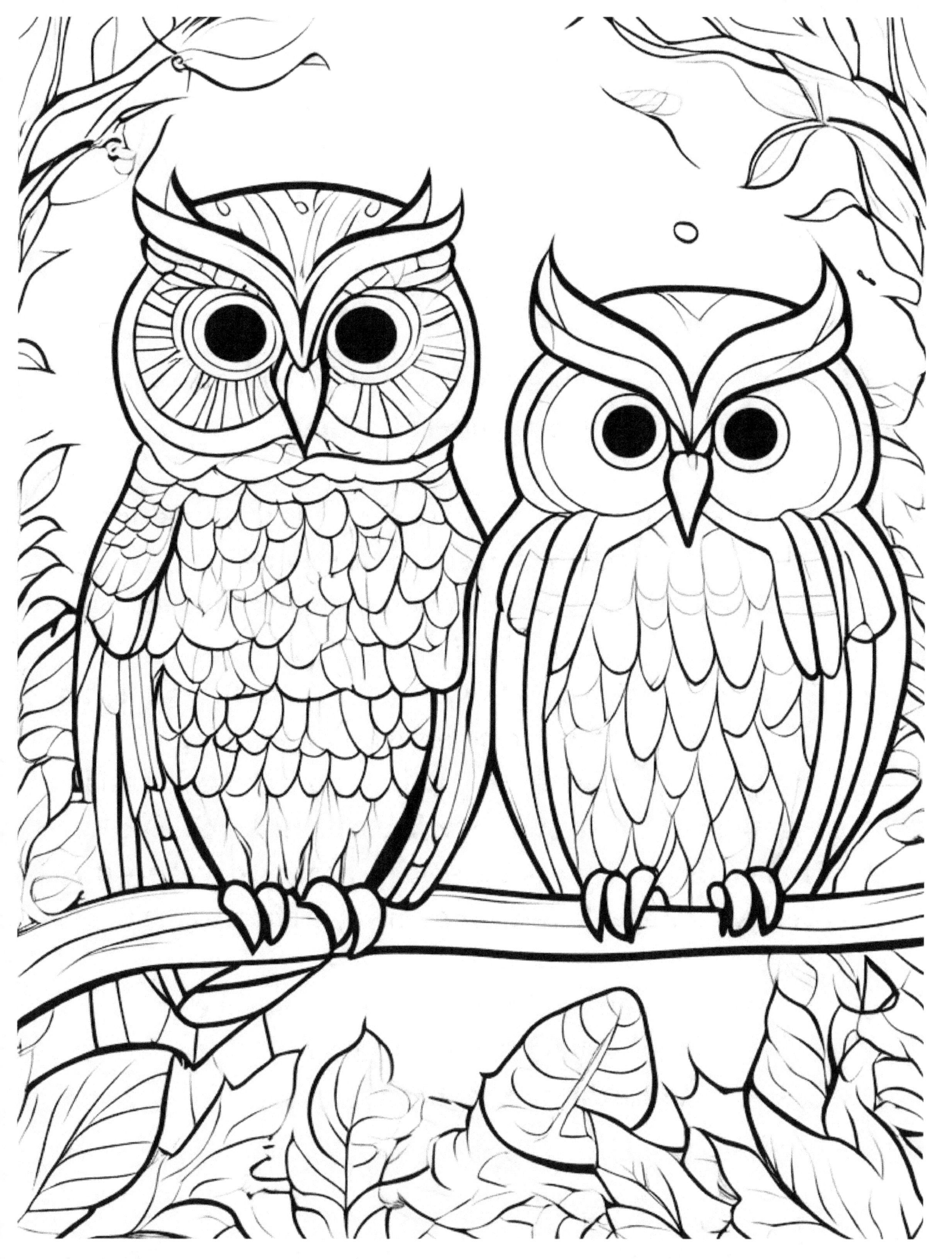

DOVE

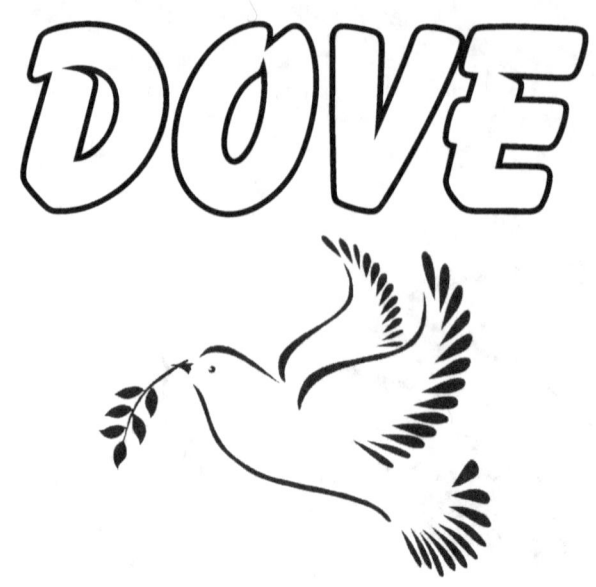

5 Characteristics of the Dove

1. Is a symbol of peace – Doves are known in many cultures as symbols of peace and harmony.
2. Has a great memory – They can recognize places and even remember human faces.
3. Can fly long distances – Doves are excellent flyers and can travel many kilometers without stopping.
4. Feeds its chicks with "crop milk" – Both the father and mother produce a nutritious liquid to feed their chicks.
5. Can find its way back home – Some homing doves are used to carry messages because they always return to their nest.

Which of these characteristics did you like learning about the most?
Write the number here: _____

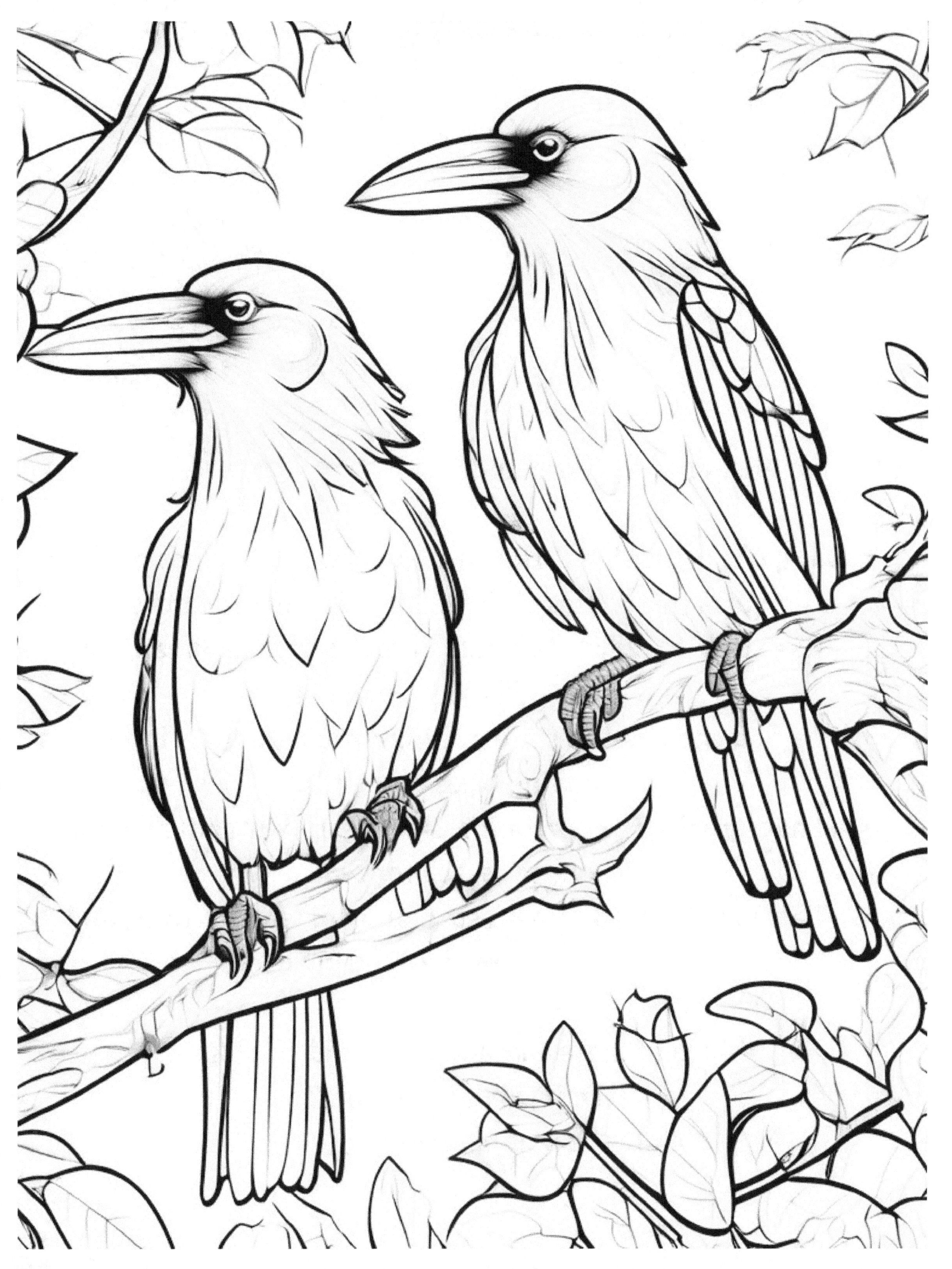

PORCUPINE

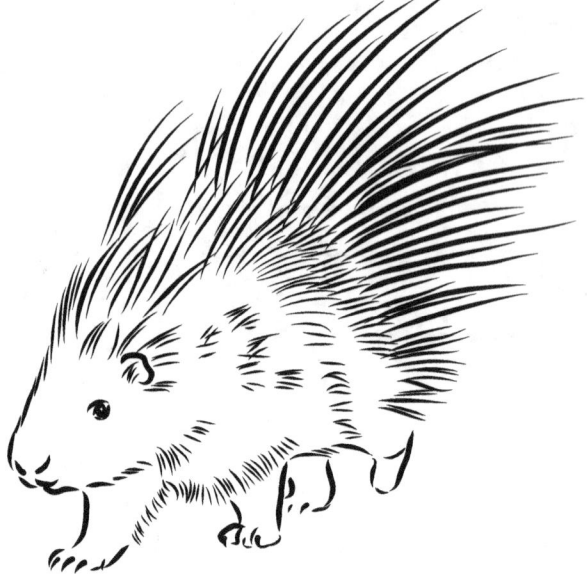

5 Characteristics of the Porcupine

1. Has quills on its skin – The porcupine has thousands of sharp quills that it uses to defend itself from predators.
2. Can shed its quills – When feeling threatened, it can shed some quills to protect itself.
3. Is a good climber – Despite its quills, the porcupine is good at climbing trees and bushes.
4. Is nocturnal – The porcupine is active at night when it goes out to search for food.
5. Eats plants – Its diet consists mainly of leaves, fruits, and tree bark.

Which of these characteristics did you like learning about the most?
Write the number here: _____

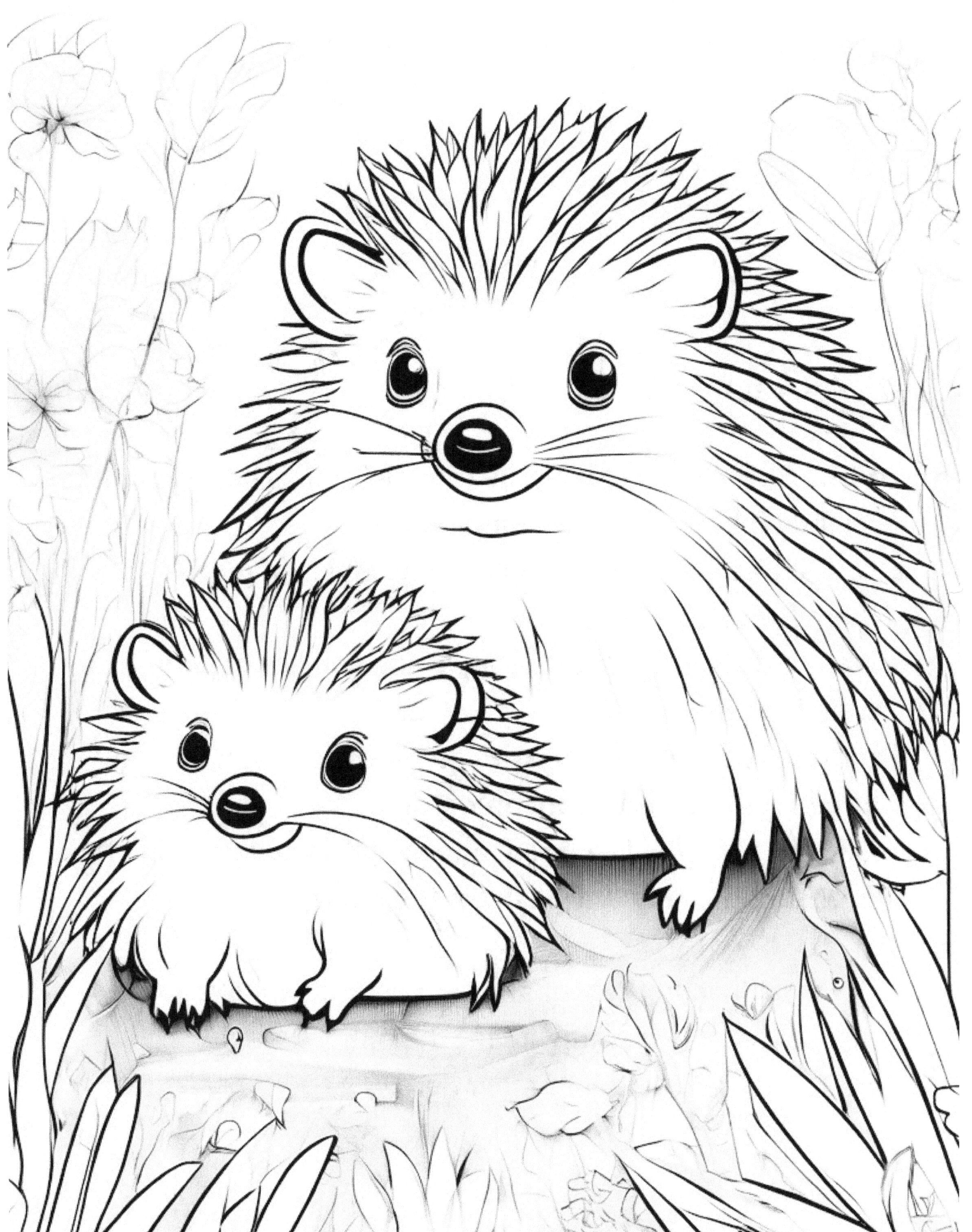

SQUIRREL

5 Characteristics of the Squirrel

1. Has a fluffy, bushy tail – The squirrel's tail is large and fluffy, helping it balance while climbing trees.
2. Loves nuts – The squirrel loves nuts and is known for storing them for the winter.
3. Is a great jumper – It's very agile and can easily jump from tree to tree.
4. Runs very fast – Squirrels are quick and can run in many directions to escape from predators.
5. Likes to store food – During autumn, they bury or hide food to ensure they have enough for the winter.

Which of these characteristics did you like learning about the most?
Write the number here: _____

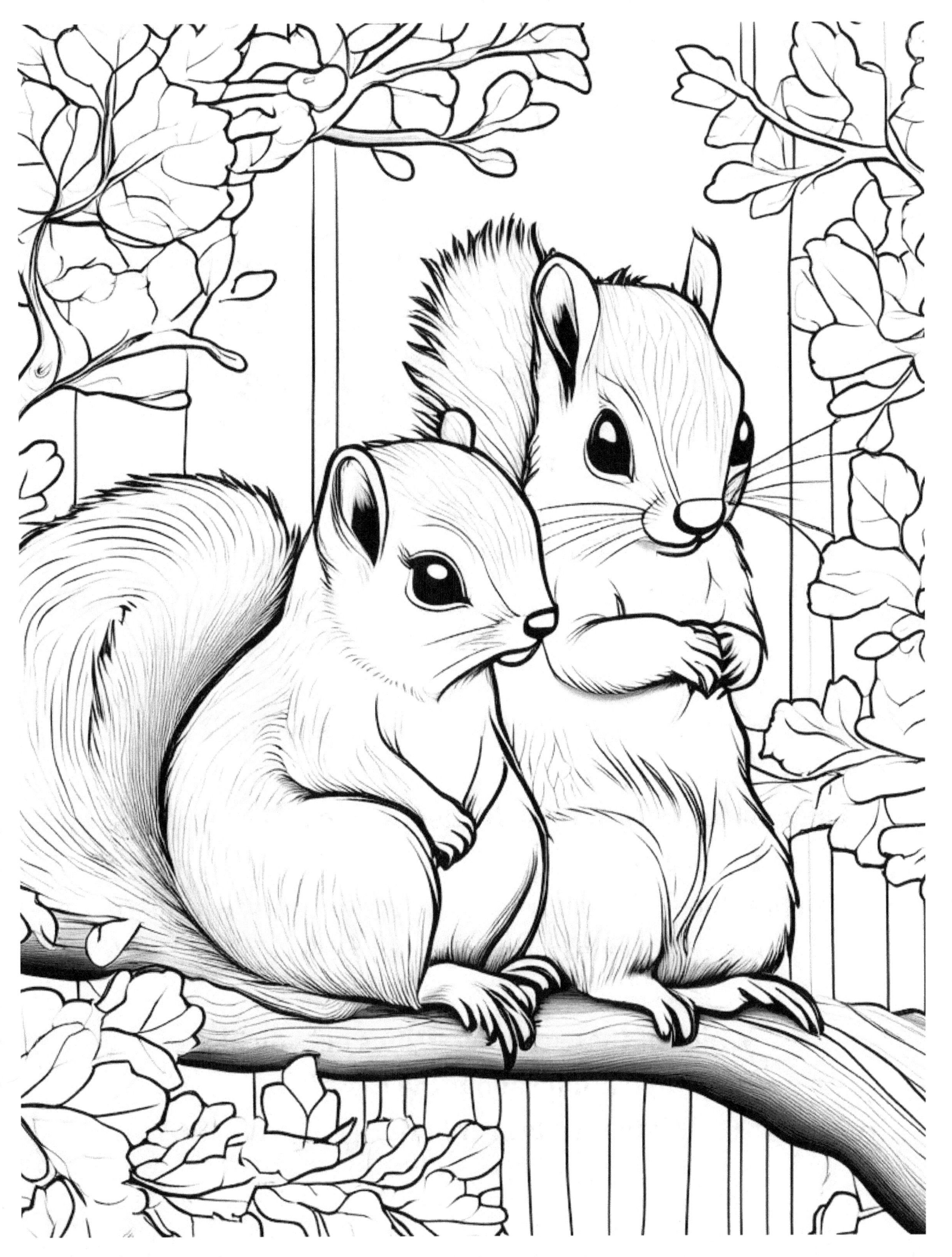

TURTLE

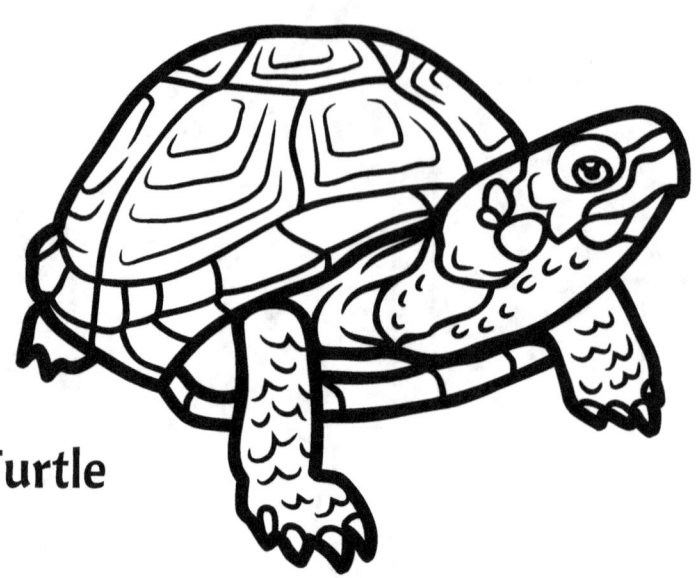

5 Characteristics of the Turtle

1. Has a hard shell – The turtle has a strong shell that protects it from dangers.
2. Is very slow – It moves slowly, but always keeps going, never giving up.
3. Lives for many years – Some turtles can live for over 100 years!
4. Likes places with water – Turtles love to live near rivers, lakes, and oceans.
5. Can breathe underwater – Some turtles can stay underwater for a long time while breathing normally.

Which of these characteristics did you like learning about the most?
Write the number here: _____

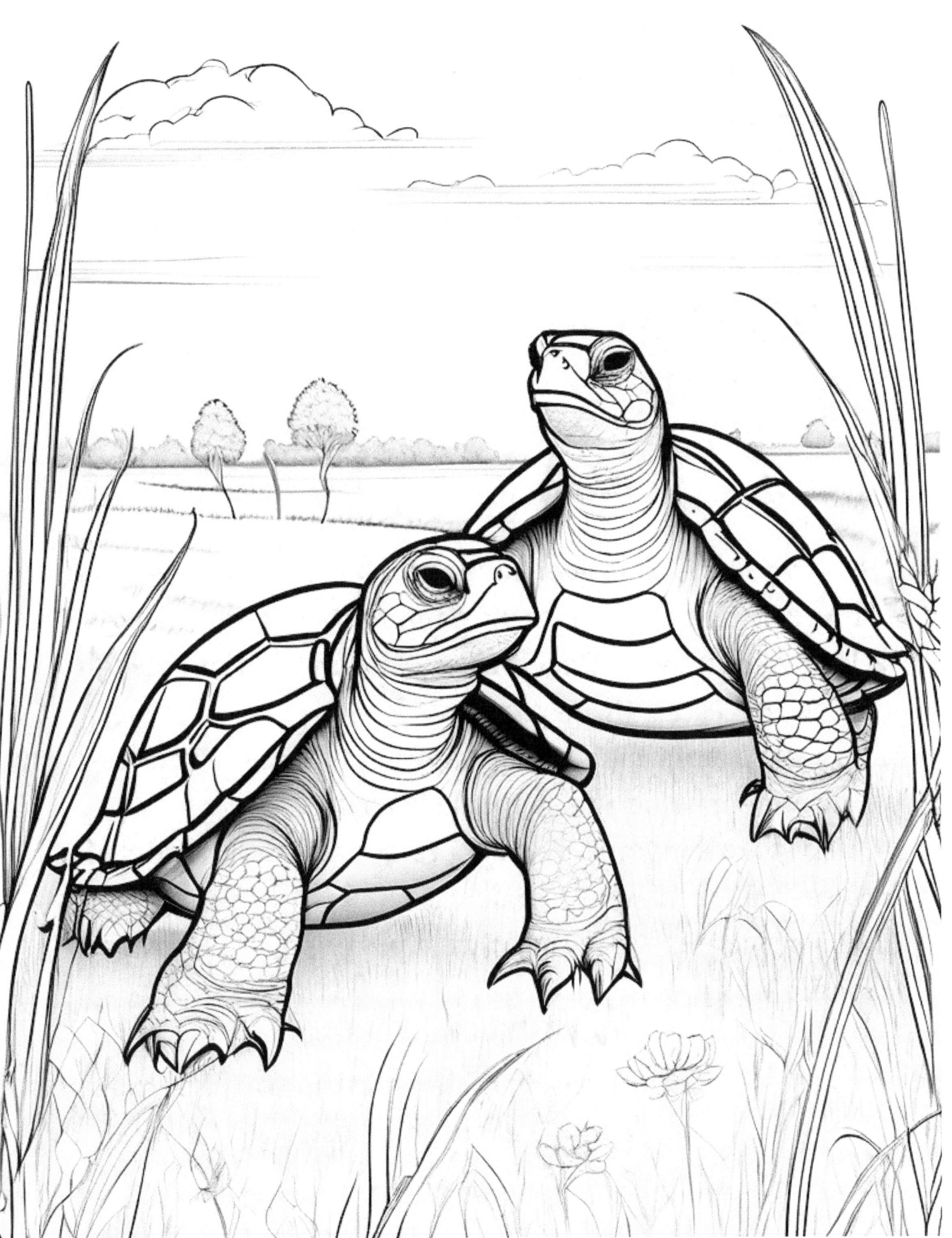

DEER

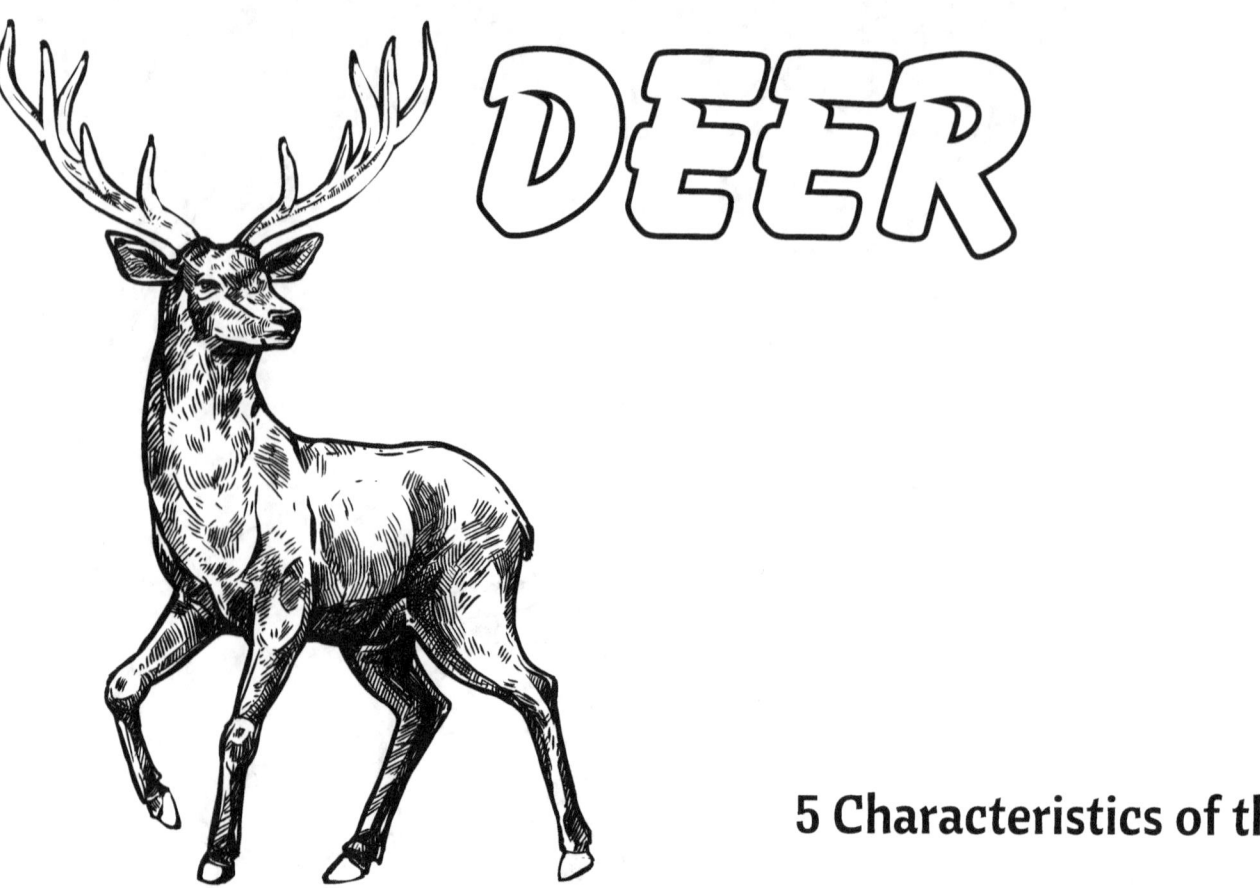

5 Characteristics of the Deer

1. Has antlers – Male deer have antlers that grow every year and are used for defense or to fight other males.
2. Is a great runner – Deer are very fast and can run at high speeds to escape from predators.
3. Has excellent vision – They have great eyesight to detect any movement, which helps them stay safe.
4. Likes to live in forests – Deer prefer habitats with lots of trees and open areas to hide in.
5. Is herbivorous – Deer mainly eat plants, such as leaves, fruits, and grasses.

Which of these characteristics did you like learning about the most?
Write the number here: _____

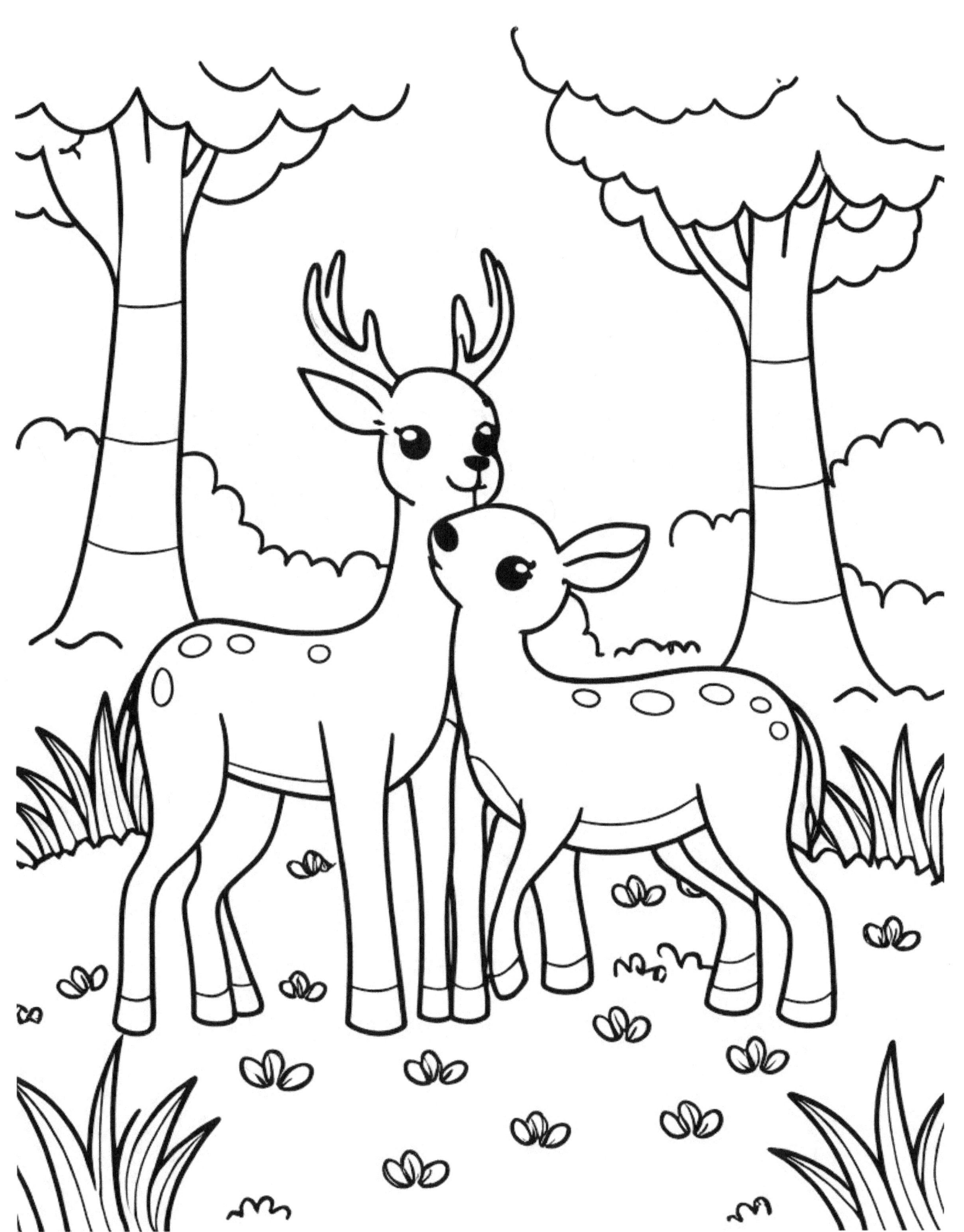

NOAH'S ARK

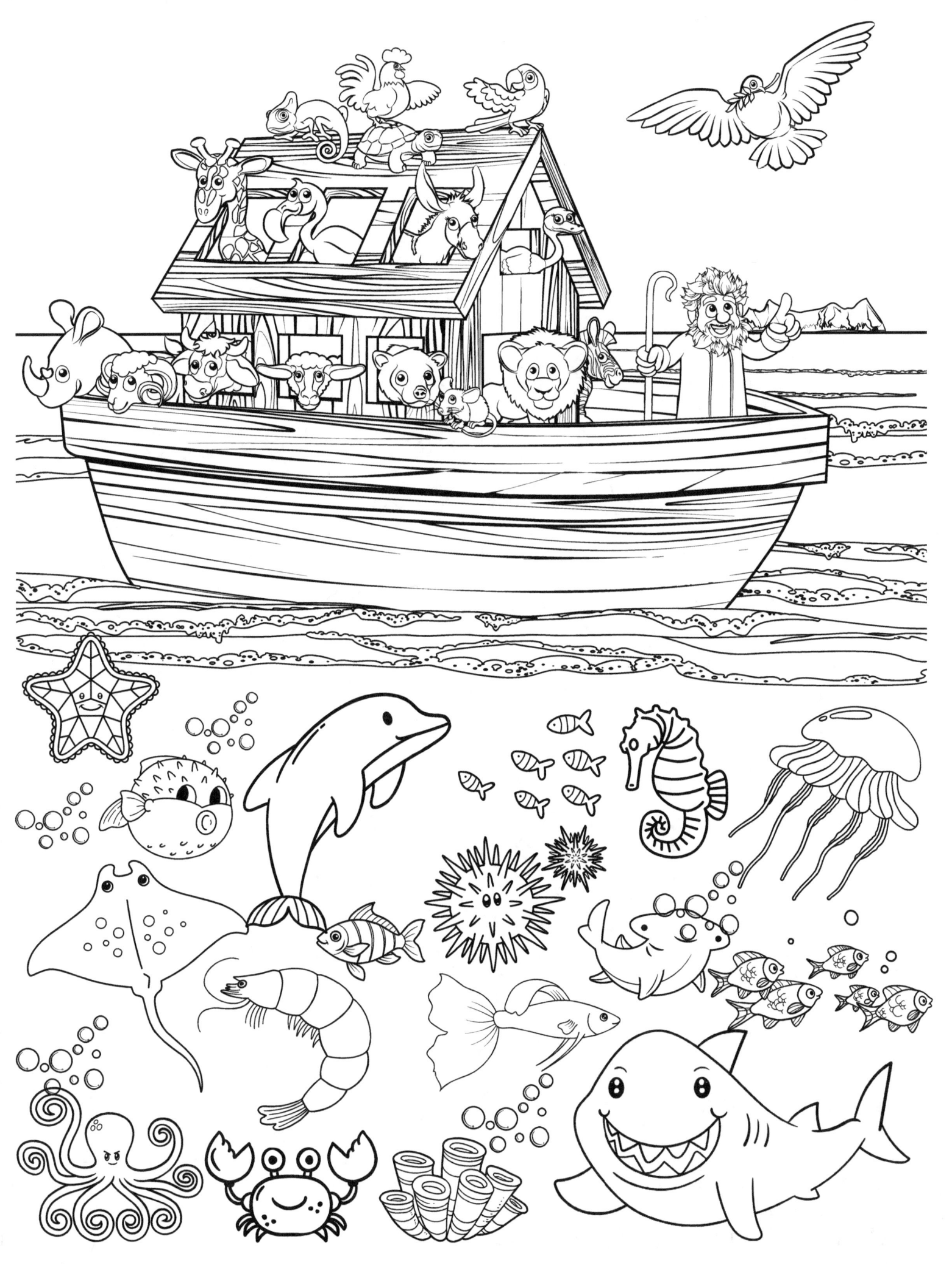

www.ingramcontent.com/pod-product-compliance
Lightning Source LLC
Chambersburg PA
CBHW062228220526
45471CB00009B/3392